VIDEO GAMES

< Design and Code Your Own Adventure >

WITH **17** PROJECTS

DISCARD

Kathy Ceceri
Illustrated by Mike Crosier

~ Latest titles in the *Build It Yourself* Series ~

Check out more titles at www.nomadpress.net

Nomad Press
A division of Nomad Communications
10 9 8 7 6 5 4 3 2 1

This book was manufactured by Marquis Book Printing,
Montmagny, Québec, Canada
September 2015, Job #115304

ISBN Softcover: 978-1-61930-300-3
ISBN Hardcover: 978-1-61930-291-4

Illustrations by Mike Crosier
Educational Consultant, Marla Conn

Questions regarding the ordering of this book should be addressed to
Nomad Press
2456 Christian St.
White River Junction, VT 05001
www.nomadpress.net

Printed in Canada.

Thanks to the following for sharing their passion for video games with me: David Schwartz of Rochester Institute of Technology's School of Interactive Games and Media, rit.edu/gccis/igm • Andy Phelps, Chris Egert, and Jenn Hinton of RIT's MAGIC center, magic.rit.edu • Jon-Paul Dyson and Shannon Symonds of the Strong Museum's International Center for the History of Electronic Games, museumofplay.org/about/icheg • Melissa Coons, Erin Wasik, Mark Christoforetti, Gabe So, and Ed Rodrigues of Vicarious Visions, vvisions.com • Tobi Saulnier and Justin Candeloro of 1st Playable, 1stplayable.com • Lance Priebe of Hyper Hippo Games, hyperhippo.ca • Amy Kraft of Monkey Bar Collective, monkeybarcollective.com • Jamey Stevenson of the Tech Valley Game Space, techvalleygamespace.com • Greg Wondra, gregwondra.wix.com/gamedev • John Ceceri III, jciii.me

And thanks to my playtesters and their families! Olive Revis • Zephan Conway • Jack Diligent • V.I. Post

CONTENTS

PS

INTERESTED IN PRIMARY SOURCES?

Look for this icon. Use a smartphone or tablet app to scan the QR code and explore more about video games! You can find a list of URLs on the Resources page.

If the QR code doesn't work, try searching the Internet with the Keyword Prompts to find other helpful sources.

3000 BCE
The *Royal Game of Ur* is buried in a tomb in present-day Iraq.

1400 BCE
Mancala is played in Egypt and Africa.

1323 CE
The board game *Senet* is buried with the mummy of King Tut in Egypt.

1700s CE
Board games are first mass produced.

1889
Nintendo is founded in Japan to make playing cards.

1903
Lizzie Magie invents *The Landlord's Game*, an early version of *Monopoly*.

1933
The board game *Scrabble* is released.

1962
Steve Russell creates the spaceship-shooter game *Spacewar!*

1939
Edward U. Condon displays a primitive game-playing computer called the Nimatron at the World's Fair in New York City.

1974
The fantasy adventure game *Dungeons & Dragons* is published.

1970s
Nintendo releases electronic games in Japan.

1972
Nolan Bushnell founds the game company Atari and releases *Pong*.

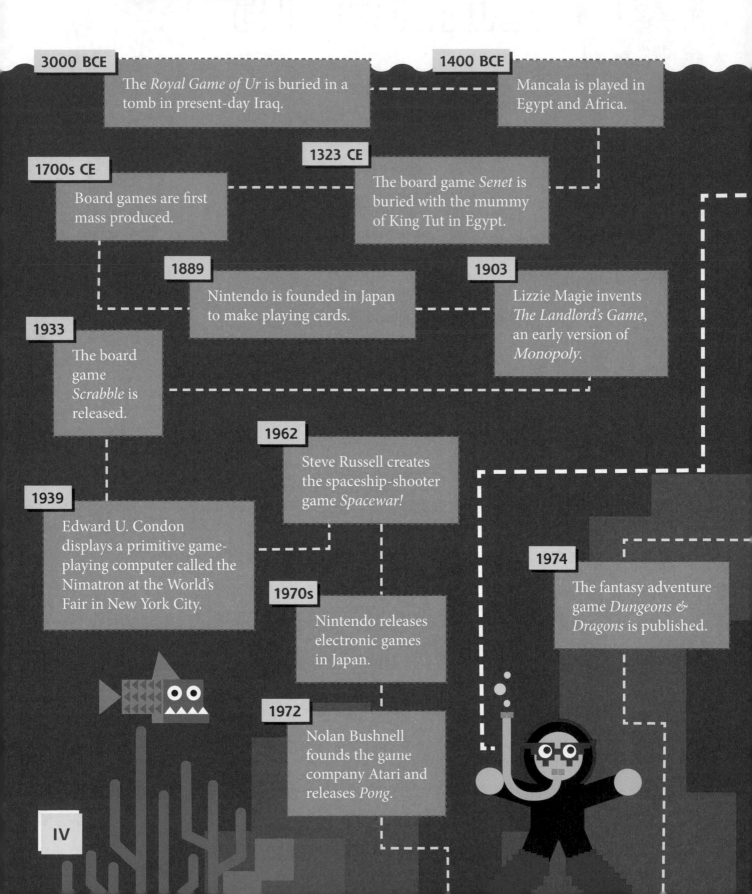

TIMELINE

1994
Sony releases the PlayStation.

1995
Microsoft's Bill Gates appears in a promotional video for Windows 95 as a character from the game *Doom.*

2001
Microsoft releases the first Xbox console.

2006
Nintendo releases the first Wii.

1997
The early mobile game *Snake* is released for cell phones.

2008
World of Warcraft becomes the most popular online multiplayer game.

1989
Nintendo comes out with the Game Boy.

1984
Russian mathematician Alexey Pajitnov invents *Tetris* to test the power of a Soviet computer.

2010
Swedish developer Markus Persson releases *Minecraft.*

2011
IBM's Watson beats two all-time champions on the TV quiz show *Jeopardy!*

1978
Milton Bradley's MicroVision becomes the first handheld game system.

2014
A film crew digs up a landfill in the Arizona desert and finds piles of the 1982 Atari game cartridges for *E.T. the Extra-Terrestrial.*

1975
Computer expert Will Crowther writes the first text-based interactive adventure, *Colossal Cave.*

2012
Wii U is released.

1977
The Atari 2600 lets users switch games using interchangeable cartridges.

v

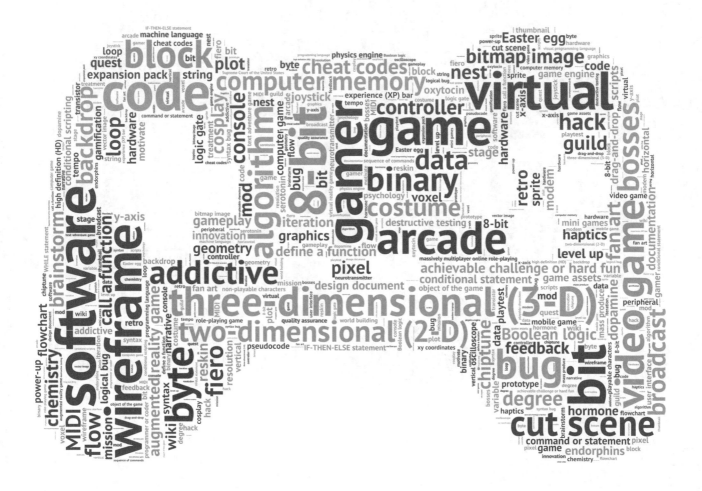

Everyone Is a Gamer!

Almost every boy and girl between the ages of 12 and 17 living in the United States has played some kind of <u>video game</u>.

Toddlers play *Doc McStuffins* games on their LeapPad tablets while their older siblings bop around to *Just Dance* on the Wii U in front of their TVs. Teenagers join multiplayer games that can last for days or weeks! Even adults can be found playing solitaire on their desktop computers or *Candy Crush Saga* on their smartphones. Wow! That's a lot of gaming!

WORDS TO KNOW

video game: a game that is played by controlling images on a screen. Also known as an electronic game or digital game.

1

VIDEO GAMES

Video games, which are also called computer games, electronic games, or digital games, have been around for a while, but they've never been as widespread as they are today. Back in the 1970s and 1980s, companies advertised home computers as learning and game machines for boys to use, although plenty of girls used them, too. Now, thanks to the availability of devices, it's easy for almost everyone to enjoy video games.

You could say that pretty much everyone is a gamer!

Think about all the ways people could be spending their free time, from watching movies to reading books to riding bikes to collecting rocks. It's pretty amazing to realize that one particular activity has captured the interest of so many different people.

BONUS POINTS

Before video games were invented, people went to **arcades** to play coin-operated games of skill. These games include pinball machines, where players use flippers to knock rolling marbles into bumpers to earn points, and Skee-Ball games, where the goal is to throw balls at a target.

WHAT DO YOU WANT TO BE WHEN YOU GROW UP?

In 2014, the game company Hasbro decided to update the job choices in *The Game of Life.* So the company did a survey that asked 400 children ages 8 to 12 in the United States, the United Kingdom, Germany, France, Mexico, South Korea, and Australia what they want to be when they grow up. The top answer? Video game designer!

WHAT IS A GAME?

To understand why gaming is so popular, it helps to know what a game really is. Here are some things you'll find in almost every game.

Interactive features. Unlike other forms of entertainment, such as comic books or movies, games make you part of the action. One thing every game has to have is a **controller** that a player uses to play the game. Each time you play it's a different experience, and the outcome of the game depends on you.

Goals. The **object of the game** might be to win or to get a high score or to advance to the highest level. In **world-building** games, the goal is to keep your characters alive and happy. The goal helps you decide what moves to make next.

Challenges. Games make you work by challenging you on your way to the goal. These have to be the right kind of challenges. If a game is too easy, players will quickly become bored. If it's too hard, they'll give up. And if only certain players can win, such as those who are richer or taller or older than the rest, then players will feel that the game is unfair.

controller: a part or device that players use to interact with a game.

object of the game: what you have to do to win or reach the final goal, also called the objective.

world-building: designing an imaginary setting for your game to take place in, including the people or creatures that live there, how they move and communicate, and what the buildings and landscape look like.

WORDS TO KNOW

The best games offer challenges that the average player can achieve with the right combination of skill, luck, strength, and knowledge. Many games also let you change the level of difficulty so that the challenge is just right for your skill level but gets harder as you get better.

Rewards and surprises. Winning a game feels awesome! But the best games also give you smaller, unexpected rewards along the way. You might get extra points for shooting down a passing UFO, temporary protection from attack, or mini games within a game that earn you useful items.

PS

DO GAMES HAVE TO BE FUN?

Video games are often thought of as pure entertainment, but they are used for other purposes as well. Early computers were sometimes taught to play chess as a way of testing how powerful they were. Games such as *Math Blaster* were used to help kids with the multiplication tables. Games such as *The Oregon Trail* took players on trips through history.

Today, some designers create serious games that they hope will make the world a better place and help people lead better lives. For example, players in *Climate Defense* try to prevent global warming by planting trees. Serious games can also be fun! The city of Melbourne, Australia, wanted to warn people to stay safe around train tracks, so it created a silly commercial that later became a game called *Dumb Ways to Die*. Colorful blobs in this game die in weird ways, such as from eating tubes of glue. And in the game *Zombies, Run!*, players get exercise in the real world while trying to fulfill **missions** and avoid the undead. You can sample some serious games on the website Games for Change.

Games for change

These little surprises make you willing to take risks and keep going when the challenges get tough.

Competition and cooperation. Many games pit players against each other or against the game itself. Some multi-player games encourage you to work together with other players in teams called guilds to fight rival gangs and enemies.

Clear rules. The rules in a game tell you what you can and cannot do. For example, you might be allowed to use a dictionary in a word game or go online to look up the answer to a trivia question. Adjusting the rules is another way to make the challenge easier or harder for different players. Mostly, however, they simply make the game fair for all players.

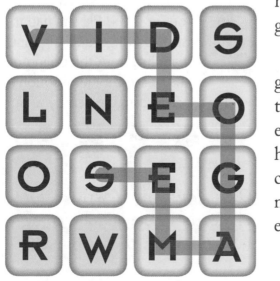

Useful items to collect. In many games, players start out with things that will help along the way. You earn more (or lose the ones you have) as the game goes along. These can include game pieces, tools, money, health points, weapons, or extra turns.

Training. Games teach you skills and strategies that can help you win. In some cases, the *real* object of a game isn't to rack up points, but to learn skills or information that are useful in the real world.

Fun. If games weren't fun to play, there wouldn't be so many gamers!

So, what's the best definition of a game? You could say that a game is a fun, challenging activity in which players compete using skill, knowledge, and luck. The point is to complete tasks and earn rewards, without breaking the rules, in order to reach the final goal.

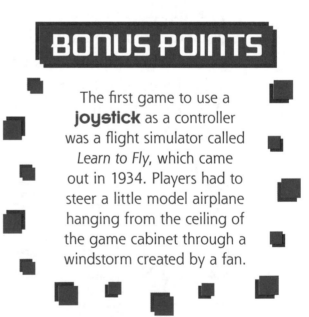

BONUS POINTS

The first game to use a **joystick** as a controller was a flight simulator called *Learn to Fly*, which came out in 1934. Players had to steer a little model airplane hanging from the ceiling of the game cabinet through a windstorm created by a fan.

Video Games: Design and Code Your Own Adventure is written for everyone who likes video games. You'll learn where games come from, how they are made today, and how to create them yourself!

Game jam activities will give you hands-on experience making games. As you work on your own games, you'll develop skills in storytelling, technical writing, communications, graphic design, computers, and teamwork. And you'll have fun doing it!

FLAVIUS
30th level Paladin

NEXT QUEST
- Clear the dungeon of Ederith's Lost Castle
- Find the Ruby Horn of Gary Gygax

Ready, player? Then hit start! Good luck!

WORDS·TO·KNOW

Game jam: a gathering of game developers to design and create games in a short period of time.

GOOD SCIENCE PRACTICES

Every good game developer keeps a game journal! Choose a notebook to use as your game journal. As you read through this book and do the activities, keep track of your ideas, your game development process, your results, and ways in which you can make your games and inventions better.

Each chapter of this book begins with an essential question to help guide your exploration of video games.

? ESSENTIAL QUESTION

Keep the question in your mind as you read the chapter. At the end of each chapter, use your game journal to record your thoughts and answers.

MAKE A CARDBOARD ARCADE GAME

IDEAS FOR SUPPLIES

lots of recycled cardboard ❖ craft materials such as pipe cleaners, straws, popsicle sticks, and bottle caps ❖ things to toss ❖ decorating supplies

In 2011, nine-year-old Caine Monroy built working cardboard versions of his favorite arcade games in his dad's auto parts shop, including a basketball toss and a tabletop soccer game with plastic army men. A customer named Nirvan Mullick liked Caine's Arcade so much, he invited lots of people to come and play. Mullick also made a short documentary about Caine's Arcade, and Caine became famous! You can watch the video here.

Caine's Arcade 🔍

Mullick also started the Imagination Foundation. The group holds a Global Cardboard Challenge every year in which kids around the world create cardboard games. In this activity, you'll design an arcade game using cardboard, tape, string, small toys, and other household items. This is fun to do with other people. You can all share your materials. Ask local appliance stores if they have any leftover cardboard boxes.

1 **Brainstorm** ideas for games to build. How might they work? Sketch out your ideas on a piece of paper and choose one to work on. Make notes and drawings to show how the different parts of the game fit together. Be sure to write out the directions so other people will know how to play the game.

WORDS TO KNOW

brainstorm: to come up with a bunch of ideas quickly and without judgment.

Easter egg: a secret message or surprise hidden in a video game for players to find.

2 Following your plans, cut out the cardboard shapes you need and put them together using tape, staples, or other fasteners. Test it to make sure it works. Are all the parts moving correctly and easily? Does your game have goals, challenges, and rewards? What are the rules? What is a good name for your game?

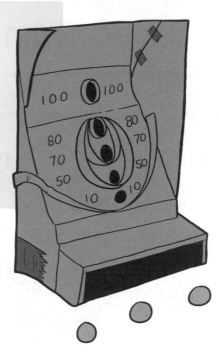

3 When your game is ready, invite friends and family to try it out! If you find problems, fix them and test it out again. Ask players to offer feedback so the next game you make is even better.

EASTER EGGS

In many video games, the designers hide little surprises known as **Easter eggs** for the players to find. The first known Easter egg was found in a 1979 game called *Adventure*. The author of the game hid the words "Created by Warren Robinett" in a secret room. It wasn't discovered until a year after the game's release! In *The Legend of Zelda: A Link to the Past*, lucky players might stumble upon the Chris Houlihan Room. Filled with jewels and other useful items, the room is named for a fan who won a contest. Easter eggs often include guest appearances by characters from other games, celebrity voices, or bonus mini games.

CHAPTER 1

Video Games and Their Roots

Games are as old as human civilization. The *Royal Game of Ur* is a 4,600-year-old board game made of rare stones and jewels. It was discovered in the tomb of a princess in the area that is now called Iraq. In Egypt, a popular board game called *Senet* was buried alongside the mummy of the boy ruler King Tut about 3,300 years ago. The game of *Go* originated in China about 4,000 years ago and is still a very popular game today!

Around the Middle East, northern Africa, and in the ruins from the Roman Empire, you can still see ancient mancala boards. They have two or more rows of holes scratched into stone to hold the pebbles or seeds that people used as playing pieces.

ESSENTIAL QUESTION

What do today's video games have in common with ancient games?

Many of these ancient games are still around today in modern form. You may even have played some of them.

The *Royal Game of Ur* evolved into the game of backgammon. If you have a checkerboard at home, flip it over. You might find a backgammon board on the back, ready to be played with the same pieces. *Parcheesi* and *Chutes and Ladders* originally came from ancient India. And chess, which has been called "the game of kings," has been played around the world for at least 1,000 years.

BONUS POINTS

Chutes and Ladders is known as *Snakes and Ladders* outside the United States.

THE MODERN ERA OF BOARD GAMES

As far back as the 1700s, paper mills and printing presses made it possible to **mass produce** games for the average family. But it wasn't until the 1900s that games became a big business.

These early, commercially made games weren't just for fun. They were meant to teach lessons or morals, although that didn't always work out as planned. In 1903, a political activist named Lizzie Magie invented *The Landlord's Game*. She hoped it would show how people could work together to help each other stay out of the poorhouse.

WORDS TO KNOW

mass produce: to manufacture large amounts of a product.

Her plan backfired. Instead, players bought up as much property as they could and tried to make other players go broke. Thirty years later, a man named Charles Darrow made his own version and called it *Monopoly*. It became the best-selling board game ever.

Chance

BE CHARLES DARROW
INVENT MONOPOLY
MAKE MILLIONS

Many of the games created in the mid-1900s are still popular today.

Candy Land, which came out in 1945, can teach preschoolers to recognize colors and to count, just like many games on tablets do today. *Battleship* was originally a pencil-and-paper game played by Russian soldiers during World War I. It was turned into a board game in 1957, the same year that *Risk*, a game of world conquest, was released.

Many early board games influenced the video games that were invented later. The 1933 crossword game *Scrabble* inspired the **mobile game** *Words with Friends*. Both *Battleship* and *Risk* became models for today's war and strategy video games.

STANG   5th
Lawful Good Paladin
AC HP
2   48

ABILITIES   SAVING THROWS
17 STR   7 POISON
9   DEX   5 WAND
13 CON   5 STONE
10 INT   4 SPELL
11 WIS   1 DRAGON
WEAPONS: ITEMS:

Cola

Cheeeos

WORDS TO KNOW

mobile game: a game that can be played on a mobile device such as a smartphone or tablet.

For video game designers, two kinds of tabletop games have been particularly important. **Role-playing games (RPG)**, especially the 1974 fantasy adventure game *Dungeons & Dragons*, led directly to video games such as *World of Warcraft* and *Final Fantasy*. And European strategy games such as 1995's *Settlers of Catan*, where players gather and trade resources to keep their colonies running, are a little bit like world-building video games such as *Civilization* and *SimCity*.

Video game designers have used almost every kind of board game for inspiration. Many game designers even make rough board game versions of possible video game ideas to see if they work.

role-playing game (RPG): a game, usually with a fantasy setting, where players' actions reflect the characters they play in the story.

WORDS TO KNOW

RISE OF THE GAME MACHINES

The earliest video games were created to run on computers. But only researchers and college students could play them because computers were so big and expensive that only laboratories could afford them.

In 1939, atomic scientist Edward U. Condon displayed a primitive game-playing computer called the Nimatron at the World's Fair in New York City. It used rows of flashing lights as game pieces, and beat almost all of the 50,000 people who played against it.

VIDEO GAMES

How do you think people reacted when they saw this first video game? Is there anything from today that is equal to this level of **innovation**?

Scientist William Higinbotham created *Tennis for Two* for visitors' day at Brookhaven National Laboratory in New York in 1958. This was the first computer game you could play on a screen. Players watched the path of a bouncing ball on an **oscilloscope**, a device that shows electrical signals as wavy lines. The screen was round and only 5 inches across.

PROGRAMMING FUN

People who worked with early computers were soon designing games for fun and sharing them with their friends. In 1962, Massachusetts Institute of Technology student Steve Russell created *Spacewar!*, a spaceship-shooting game. It quickly spread to colleges around the country. *Colossal Cave,* a **text adventure game** written in 1975 by computer expert and cave explorer Will Crowther, was based on *Dungeons & Dragons* and the real-life Mammoth Cave in Kentucky. Players had to find their way through what the game called "a maze of twisty little passages, all alike," with only written directions to guide them. The game had no images at all. Similar games with names such as *Adventure* and *Zork* became so popular that they were included with the first desktop computers built for homes and offices.

The idea of hooking up a game **console** to a TV set so you could play at home came from a television engineer named Ralph Baer. Often called the "father of video games," Baer built the first experimental console, now known as the "Brown Box," in 1967. He sold his idea to a company called Magnavox, which released the Odyssey, the first multiplayer, multiprogram video game system for home use, in 1972.

> **console:** a specialized computer used to play video games on a TV screen.
>
> **WORDS TO KNOW**

The Odyssey was extremely primitive. All of its games were built into the machine, so you couldn't add more. But the Odyssey represented the beginning of the home video game industry. Baer went on to invent many other electronic toys, including the electronic game *Simon*, which flashes patterns of light on colored buttons that players must repeat to move to the next level.

BONUS POINTS

In 1997, an IBM supercomputer called Deep Blue made headlines for beating world chess Grandmaster Garry Kasparov in a match. And in 2011, IBM's Watson proved that supercomputers could understand human speech—and even clues with jokes in them—when it beat two all-time champions on the TV quiz show *Jeopardy!*

Baer was still working on new games when he died in 2014 at the age of 92.

15

Around the same time that video games began to move into homes, the first video arcade machines appeared. In 1970, Nolan Bushnell created *Computer Space* based on the computer game *Spacewar!* The game was housed in a sleek, brightly colored cabinet that looked like a control panel on a spaceship.

Later, Bushnell founded the video game company Atari. Its first game was *Pong,* released in 1972. Like the oscilloscope game *Tennis for Two,* in *Pong* players made a white square bounce back and forth between two lines. Although extremely simple, *Pong* set off the Golden Age of video arcade games.

Meanwhile, home consoles kept improving. With more processing power and enhanced controls, they were able to deliver better **graphics** and more interesting gameplay.

The Atari 2600, released in 1977, was the first major console to let you switch games using interchangeable cartridges. It also featured a joystick and switches that let you set the difficulty.

BONUS POINTS

Have you seen the animated film *Wreck-It Ralph*? Many characters from actual classic games of the past, including *Q*Bert, Sonic the Hedgehog, Pac-Man, Frogger,* and *Space Invaders*, appear in this movie, which is about an old video arcade game.

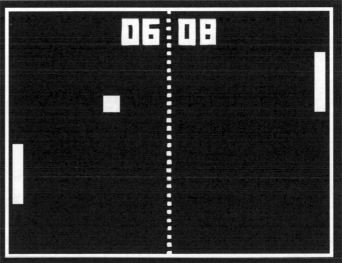

WORDS TO KNOW

graphics: the images on a computer screen, including a game's characters and background.

By 1982, the Commodore 64 home computer was the most popular game platform in the United States.

Desktop computers were becoming available for the home and many were used for gaming.

In 1981, a century-old Japanese game company called Nintendo arrived in the United States and soon dominated the video game market. Nintendo's arcade game *Donkey Kong* became the hottest-selling coin-operated machine around. Created by Nintendo artist Shigeru Miyamoto, *Donkey Kong* introduced a little workman named Jumpman. Today, that character is better known as Mario.

One of the reasons Nintendo was so successful was because the company took game design seriously. How a game looked and played was considered just as important as the technology used to run it. This attitude helped Nintendo games such as *Metroid*, *Super Mario Bros.*, and *The Legend of Zelda* become instant classics.

PHONE HOME!

Atari's 1982 game *E.T. the Extra-Terrestrial* is often called the worst video game ever made. In fact, many blame it for the slump that hit the entire video game industry at that time. For many years, video game fans heard rumors that Atari had buried unsold copies of *E.T.* in the New Mexico desert. No one knew if the stories were true. Then, in 2014, a film crew dug up a landfill and found piles of crushed, dust-covered cartridges! Fans spent thousands of dollars buying them on eBay. Cartridges were even donated to the Smithsonian Museum in Washington, D.C., and the International Center for the History of Electronic Games at the Strong Museum of Play in Rochester, New York.

In 1985, the Nintendo Entertainment System (NES) brought advanced graphics, animation, and sound to home consoles and pulled the entire video game industry out of a slump that had started around 1982. NES set the stage for the Sony PlayStation in 1994 and Microsoft's Xbox in 2001.

The first handheld system was Milton Bradley's MicroVision, which came out in 1978. The idea didn't take off, though, until Nintendo came out with the Game Boy in 1989.

BONUS POINTS

Russian cosmonaut Aleksandr Serebrov brought a Game Boy with *Tetris* to the space station *Mir* in 1993. You can play a version of *Tetris* at this website.

PS

Free Tetris 🔍

Once handheld games arrived, players could carry their games wherever they went.

Included with the first Game Boy was a free puzzle game called *Tetris*. Russian mathematician Alexey Pajitnov had invented *Tetris* in 1984 as a way to test the power of a Soviet computer. *Tetris* was an immediate success and many consider it the most perfect video game ever invented. What do you think?

Using computer networks to play with other gamers also became a growing trend. In 1993, *Doom* let players in different places compete in matches over primitive computer networks. Then in 1999, Sega released the Dreamcast, the first console with a modem built into it. This is a device that lets you connect to the Internet. That was followed by Xbox Live in 2002, which let you use the same identity in different online games and allowed you to post your scores for other players to see.

With today's **massively multiplayer online (MMO)** role-playing games such as *World of Warcraft*, millions of people around the world can play the same game at the same time. *Club Penguin*, a

massively multiplayer online (MMO): an online role-playing game in which large numbers of players all take part in the same game.

WORDS TO KNOW

MMO game for kids owned by Disney, lets you create your own penguin avatar, play minigames, and chat with other players. *Club Penguin* has had more than 200 million registered users.

Smaller, independent game companies, called indies, have taken advantage of the Internet, too. Steam, an online gaming platform, makes it possible for these indies to reach 35 million players, who can download any game instantly to their home PCs.

The invention of mobile games has meant that people no longer need special devices. Anyone with a cell phone can play anytime, anywhere. Early mobile games included 1997's *Snake*, which was just a wiggling line you chased around a black-and-green screen.

In 2009, the touch screen opened up a whole new way to interact with games, such as *Plants* vs. *Zombies*, on your smartphone or tablet.

Other advances in game consoles included Nintendo's Wii from 2006, which let you control games with everything from a golf club to a guitar. The Xbox Kinect in 2010 had audio and motion sensors that let you put yourself in the game just by moving your body around.

Newer games do even more to blur the lines between make-believe and the real world. **Augmented reality games** insert real-world images into the game environment or interact with real-world objects. **Toys-to-life** games such as *Skylanders* and *Disney Infinity* use special action figures that the console can scan. The figures then become playable characters in the game.

In 2015, the new *Lego Dimensions* game featured **minifigs** from *The Simpsons*, *Scooby-Doo*, *Doctor Who*, *Back to the Future*, and other classic TV shows and movies. A level pack based on *Portal 2* included Lego versions of a turret, a companion cube, and the heroine Chell.

One of the most exciting new developments in game technology is the **virtual reality game**. Players wear screens over their eyes that wrap around like giant sunglasses to make them feel as though they are inside the game itself.

THE WIDE WORLD OF GAMES

Today, video games rule the home entertainment world. They're exciting, colorful, and interactive, and there are many  different kinds to choose from. Game developers and fans divide games into categories according to what they are about and how you play them. Here are some of the most common categories.

- **Puzzle games** such as *Tetris, Pac-Man,* and *Candy Crush* involve stacking blocks, finding the way through a maze, or matching up tiles to clear the board.

- **Action/adventure games** such as *The Legend of Zelda* send players on missions to find a treasure or dcfcat an enemy.

- **Platformers** such as *Super Mario Bros.* are games where the characters jump, climb, or slide from one platform to another to reach the goal. They include side-scrollers, which are games where the background moves sideways to make it seem as though the action takes place in a world that is wider than the screen.

- **Strategy games** give players control of armies or empires, as in the game *Sid Meier's Civilization.*

- **Simulation games** such as *Minecraft* and *The Sims* let players design the world within the game.

- **Sports games,** including *Madden Football* and *Wii Sports,* let players play sports without leaving their homes.

- **Racing games** such as *Gran Turismo* involve racing cars, go-karts, or other vehicles. Flight simulators do the same thing in planes, helicopters, or rockets.

- **Fighting games** such as *Super Smash Bros. Melee* feature large numbers of characters battling it out using martial arts, boxing, or wrestling moves.

- **Shooting games** include first-person shooters (FPS), where the player "sees" through the eyes of the main character, and rail shooters, where the player's character moves through the scene automatically, as if rolling along a railroad track.

- **Edutainment games,** such as those on the site Brain Pop, are designed to teach traditional school subjects.

You could say there's a video game for every person, no matter what they're looking for. But what makes games so appealing in the first place? In the next chapter, we'll look at how video games affect the brain.

BONUS POINTS

Author J.K. Rowling played *Minesweeper* on her computer as a break between writing chapters of the Harry Potter series of books.

CONSIDER THE ESSENTIAL QUESTION

Write your thoughts about this chapter's Essential Question in your game journal, using information you've gathered from reading and knowledge you may already have. Share it with other students and friends. Did you all come up with the same answers? What is different? Do this for every chapter.

? **ESSENTIAL QUESTION**

What do today's video games have in common with ancient games?

BUILD YOUR OWN MANCALA GAME

IDEAS FOR SUPPLIES

egg carton, 1 dozen size ❖ *2 small plastic cups, such as recycled yogurt containers* ❖ *decorating supplies* ❖ *48 playing pieces, such as pebbles, large beans, or pasta shapes*

Strategy games, such as chess and backgammon, use math and logic to help players figure out their next moves. That's why they're simple to learn but become more challenging as your skill increases. One of the oldest strategy games is mancala, which means "to move" in Arabic. Mancala is believed to have been created in Egypt more than 3,000 years ago and it is still popular throughout the Middle East, Africa, Asia, and the Caribbean today.

A mancala board has two or more rows of holes, and a cup or "store" at each end. The boards range from very plain to very decorative. Fancier boards were sometimes carved from wood in the shape of boats, fish, or crocodiles. Some had legs or human figures to hold them up. You can make your own board and learn how to play mancala on page 26.

1 Cut the cover off the egg carton. The bottom part is your playing board. Tape the cups to the ends to make the stores that hold captured game pieces.

2 If you want your board to have legs, tape cardboard tubes to the bottom. When finished, smooth out the surface with extra layers of tape.

3 Paint your board, including inside the cups. When it's dry, decorate it! Flip to page 26 for game instructions.

23

TASTY *TETRIS* TREATS

IDEAS FOR SUPPLIES

microwave oven ❖ *waxed paper* ❖ *10-ounce bag large marshmallows*
❖ *3 microwave-safe mixing bowls* ❖ *7 cups crispy rice cereal* ❖
3½ tablespoons butter ❖ *cooking spray or cooking oil* ❖ *soup
spoons* ❖ *food coloring (red, yellow, blue, and green)*

**Tetris was inspired by a puzzle called pentominoes. Its object was
to fit together different shapes made up of five boxes put together
in different ways. The shapes in *Tetris*, known as tetriminoes,
each contain four boxes. They come in seven varieties:**

- yellow squares
- light blue rods
- purple Ts

- orange Ls
- dark blue
  reverse Ls

- red Zs
- green
  reverse Zs

As random pieces slowly fall from the top of the screen, they stack up along
the bottom. Players shift and rotate them as they fall so they fit together with
no gaps. When a row fills up with no gaps, it disappears and the player earns
points. Unfinished rows pile up until they reach the top of the screen and the
game is over. These marshmallow *Tetris* Treats will disappear so fast you'll
never have to worry about losing the game.

1 Use a ruler to draw a 4-inch square and a 6-inch-by-4-inch rectangle
on a piece of paper. Divide them into boxes by drawing a grid of lines 1
inch apart. Cover your drawings with a large sheet of waxed paper.

2 In a bowl, combine seven marshmallows and ½ tablespoon butter.
Heat in the microwave on high for one minute. Stir until smooth and
creamy. If needed, heat it again in 10 second bursts, stirring each time
until just creamy.

3 Add yellow food coloring and stir until evenly mixed. Add more coloring if needed.

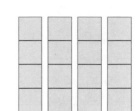

4 Add 1 cup of cereal and mix. Use cooking spray to keep the marshmallow mixture from sticking to the spoon or your hands.

5 Scoop the cereal mixture onto the square waxed paper. Press the mixture into a layer about ½-inch thick, following the outline of the square.

6 Fold the waxed paper around the edges and flatten the sides with a ruler. Use the thin edge of the ruler to press the grid lines into the cereal shape, following the patterns shown here. Place in freezer.

7 Repeat steps 2–6 with each color. Use the square waxed paper for the yellow, orange, purple, light blue, and dark blue colors. Use the rectangle for the red and green colors.

8 Remove the first square from the freezer. If it's too stiff, allow it to warm up for a few minutes. Divide the square into individual tetriminoes with a knife. Make squares, rods, T shapes, L shapes, and Z shapes. Repeat with each color. Arrange your pieces on a cookie sheet or tray by fitting different pieces together, just as in a game of *Tetris*! Cover with waxed paper and freeze until ready to serve.

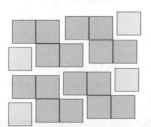

LEARN HOW TO PLAY MANCALA

1 Place the board between the players with one store on each side. The row closest to you is yours. When you capture pieces, they go in the store on your right.

2 To start, players put four playing pieces in each hole. Choose any hole on your side of the board and pick up all the pieces in it. Going counter-clockwise, drop one piece in the next hole. Keep going, dropping one piece in each hole, including your store, until you run out.

3 If your last piece falls in your own store, go again. Always skip over your opponent's store. If your last piece falls in an empty hole on your side, capture that piece, plus any pieces in the neighboring hole on your opponent's side, and place them in your store.

4 Continue taking turns until one player empties all the holes on their side of the board. That player captures any leftover pieces on their opponent's side of the board, too. The player with the most pieces wins!

MANCALA STRATEGY TIPS

To win at mancala, you must get the most pieces for yourself while blocking your opponent from getting any. Should you move your pieces from a hole that will land you in your store for an extra turn? Should you take advantage of an empty hole to capture the pieces opposite? The better your math skills, the better your mancala skills. To learn more about mancala strategy, try playing against a computer. The free online game *Mancala Snails* was developed in 2002 by Lance Priebe, who later created *Club Penguin*.

You can read an interview with Priebe in Chapter 3 and play *Mancala Snails* here.

CHAPTER 2:
Why Do We Play Games?

Most people think of games as something you do when you want a break from real life. But there are many reasons to play games. It can be a good way to connect with your friends. Competing with other players and watching your gaming skills grow can build your confidence. And it feels great to complete a game successfully! In fact, a well-designed game can actually make you want to work harder. There's a lot more to playing games than just killing time!

Game designers pay attention to what makes games popular. For clues, they look at classic games that have been around for generations. Game companies also turn to science for help. Used wisely, this information can help make games more fun, interesting, and educational.

? ESSENTIAL QUESTION

How does a video game make you want to keep playing?

27

WORDS TO KNOW

psychology: the study of how people think, behave, and feel.

Game companies use what they know about games and their effect on the brain in ways you might not realize.

Are games a harmless way to test our skills in a make-believe realm? A useful educational tool? A danger to society? Let's look at the pros and cons of video games and discover why some people consider them a new type of art form with the power to change the world.

GAME BRAIN

Have you ever become so absorbed by a game that the outside world seems to vanish? Or felt a sudden rush of excitement that made you want to shout, "Yes!" when you beat a tough challenge?

One major reason people love video games has to do with human **psychology**.

BONUS POINTS

Jane McGonigal helped design one of the first alternate reality games, *I Love Bees*, a mystery used to advertise the game *Halo 2*.

According to game designer and researcher Jane McGonigal, games fill an important psychological need in people's lives. And they do it even better than real life. You know that good feeling you get when you ace a test or spend hours perfecting a skateboard move?

Psychologists use the word *flow* to describe that calm, focused state where every move seems perfect. And that fist-pumping thrill is what game experts call *fiero*—the Italian word for "pride." Feelings such as flow and fiero are reasons players keep coming back for more.

How can a game cause such strong feelings? It has to do with **chemistry**. The human brain has evolved to increase your chances of survival. Way back when your ancestors still lived in caves, their brains released chemicals to help them stalk a gazelle for dinner or run from a ravenous mountain lion. Those are the same kinds of feelings you get when you play a game.

chemistry: the science of how substances interact, combine, and change.

hack: finding a new and different way to use or control something.

dopamine: a chemical in the brain that improves your mood and lowers stress.

neurotransmitter: a chemical that carries signals between parts of the brain.

WORDS TO KNOW

Game companies hire psychologists to tell them how to "**hack** the brain" to make their games more popular. To do this, they set up conditions that cause your brain to release certain brain chemicals.

The most common of these chemicals is **dopamine**. This **neurotransmitter** sends signals to your brain to help you focus. Dopamine is released when the brain finds the correct answer to a problem.

Researchers have used medical imaging machines to watch teenagers' brains while they play video games. They found that dopamine levels spike upward when a player gets an unexpected reward. It's one way you learn and remember.

29

Dopamine works best when your chances of doing well aren't too high or too low.

If you're sure to win, your brain doesn't need to focus. If you're likely to lose, your brain saves its energy for a challenge where the odds are more in your favor. To get the biggest dopamine boost, you need a mental task that's the right level of difficulty. Neurologists refer to this as an **achievable challenge**. Game designers call it "hard fun."

Other chemicals are involved, too. A **hormone** known as **oxytocin** makes you happy when you're with people that you like. It also works when you play games online with friends or look at pictures of cute baby animals.

The neurotransmitter **serotonin** makes you alert and puts you in a good mood. It is produced in response to light, even the light of a computer screen. **Endorphins**, another type of neurotransmitter, relieve stress and mask physical pain by creating feelings of wellness.

Laughing, crying, physical exercise, and eating spicy food all release endorphins. Think about that the next time you're deciding what to have for dinner!

PSYCHOLOGICAL MOTIVATION

A game expert named Tom Chatfield came up with seven main ways that games tap into the brain's own chemical reward system to make players want to keep playing.

Experience points. Often displayed as a progress bar, **experience points** (XP) show how far along you are toward reaching your final goal. Your brain gets a sense of satisfaction when a job is completed, so watching your points add up on a bar can be a stronger form of motivation than piling up badges. Experience points can include all kinds of achievements, not just points scored or enemies vanquished.

Short- and long-term goals. One way to make any kind of big goal more do-able is to break it down into smaller goals. Games do this by creating different levels that you move through as you gain more XP. Each time you **level up**, the game gets harder and your character grows stronger.

Rewards for effort. Instead of punishing you for failing, games reward you for trying. That encourages you to try new ideas until you eventually succeed.

Feedback. The best way to tell whether you've made a good move or a bad one is to get immediate **feedback**. Seeing the results of your decision right away reinforces what works and helps you learn quickly from mistakes.

experience points (XP): points you accumulate toward your goal, often shown as a long narrow bar.

level up: to achieve the next level by earning a certain amount of XP.

feedback: information about how you are doing.

WORDS TO KNOW

FLAVIUS
30th level Paladin

NEXT QUEST
• Clear the dungeon of Ederith's Lost Castle
• Find the Ruby Horn of Garg Gygax

Unexpected rewards. Dopamine really lights up the brain when there's a surprise involved! A game that keeps you guessing makes you pay attention to what you're doing.

Teachable moments. Dopamine can increase your memory for a short period of time, which makes it easier to learn new things. Video game players are confronted with challenges when their brains are primed to tackle the problem.

Games can be designed to present you with new information when dopamine levels are highest. This helps you improve more quickly.

Multiplayer mode. Interacting with other people is another way to make you feel good. That's why it's more fun when games let you work with and compete against other people.

HOW GAMES HELP YOU LEARN

Games can change your brain's physical structure as well as your brain chemistry. A German study in 2013 asked a group of adults to play *Super Mario 64* for half an hour every day. After two months, the brains of grown-up gamers had more gray matter than average. Gray matter is associated with processing information.

Certain parts of the brain showed the biggest change. These include the areas that control finding your way around, developing strategy, memory, and quick-hand movements.

gamification: adding game elements to another kind of activity to make it more fun or appealing.

Other kinds of changes can be seen without even looking at the brain directly. A 2003 study at the University of Rochester found that people who seldom played games did better on vision tests after a week of playing the World War II action game *Medal of Honor*.

BONUS POINTS

Adults use video games as learning tools, too. The free website Duolingo uses reward points and experience bars to help people learn foreign languages. The online game website Lumosity claims to help older people prevent their brains from slowing down.

That's why some experts believe **gamification** can be a powerful tool for learning. More and more schools are using video games in the classroom. The math app *Dragon Box* turns a difficult subject such as algebra into a fun puzzle game by teaching players to balance equations using fish, tomatoes, and fireflies instead of numbers.

virtual: a computer version of something real.

However, educational games are not always very educational. Some are full of information, but they don't really hold the interest of players. Other games are fun, but not great at teaching. For example, students who played a shooting game meant to teach multiplication facts discovered they could win by simply firing random numbers until the right answer appeared!

Some teachers are using games such as *Minecraft* to show students famous buildings, including the Roman Colosseum, and then having them create their own virtual models.

BONUS POINTS

In New York City, an experimental public school called Quest to Learn uses games as its main method of teaching. Teachers use existing games, such as *The Sims*, or create their own original board games. Even report cards have a game slant— instead of letter grades, students try to move up from novice to expert.

PS

MILITARY GAMERS

Even the U.S. military uses games to attract and train new recruits. In 2002, it created a free game called *America's Army* to interest young adults in joining. The game *Virtual Battlespace 2* helps prepare soldiers for explosions, ambushes, and other dangers they might face in a real-life war zone. The FBI and local police also use games to teach their staff how to protect computer networks and handle prison riots. You can watch a preview of *Virtual Battlespace 2* here.

Virtual Battlespace 2 🔍

DO VIDEO GAMES HAVE A DARK SIDE?

addictive: causing a strong and harmful need to do something.

WORDS TO KNOW

It's important for game designers to think about the effect of games on players' brains. When they're successful, the result can be a game that's exciting and helps your brain grow.

But some games are so good at triggering the brain's reward center that they become **addictive**. Video game addiction can make you want to play all the time, even when playing gets in the way of other important areas of your life, such as eating, sleeping, and doing homework.

Playing games can also change your brain's structure in negative ways. A study done in China in 2011 looked at college students who played the online game *World of Warcraft* for 10 hours a day or more. These brains of these students had less gray matter than students who played for only two hours a day.

There are also claims that first-person shooters, war simulations, and other violent games cause people to commit acts of violence in the real world. A direct connection has never been proven or disproven, but the possibility of a connection is troubling.

VIDEO GAMES

WORDS TO KNOW

in-app purchase: an item that you buy with real money to use in video games.

microtransaction: a very small online payment.

What studies have shown is that playing video games can change the way you behave toward other people.

In 2014, a scientist at the University of Illinois had 300 college students play a space-themed shooter game. Each student was assigned to play as one of three characters—a good guy, a bad guy, or a plain circle. Then the researcher asked the students to help with a taste test. Each student received a cup of chocolate sauce and a cup of super-hot chili sauce. They were told to choose one for the next student to taste. Those who had just played the game as the bad guy were twice as likely to choose the painfully spicy chili. Those who had played as good guys did the opposite.

BUYER BEWARE!

Free-to-play mobile games don't cost anything to start playing. But after a while, they offer to sell you special items for your characters or extra abilities to help you beat your friends' high scores. Almost one quarter of all kids who play mobile games have made **in-app purchases** without adult permission. Even console games you've already paid for sometimes ask players to make **microtransactions** to buy bonus items. Those items cost real-world money! And those purchases can quickly add up to hundreds of dollars. In 2014, both Apple and Google agreed to pay back millions of dollars to families whose children had made in-app purchases. Amazon changed the way its in-app purchases work after the U.S. government sued the company. Be aware of the tricks game companies use, and put controls on your games to avoid spending money by accident. Check your device settings or go to Amazon, iTunes, and the Google Play Store for instructions on limiting in-app purchases.

Video games might not turn kids into bad people, but they do affect how you think. And video games can be addictive. That's one reason families need to talk about which games are right for each person and set limits on playing time.

BANNING AND RATING GAMES

In 1992, the arcade game *Mortal Kombat* was the most popular game around. In this game, players fought to the death and losers were ripped limb from limb! By the time a home console version was released a year later, critics had become alarmed.

At a press conference, U.S. Senator Joseph Lieberman told reporters, "We're not talking *Pac-Man* or *Space Invaders* anymore. We're talking about video games that glorify violence and teach children to enjoy inflicting the most gruesome forms of cruelty imaginable."

Congress held hearings on video game violence. Lawmakers threatened to create a government board to oversee the video game industry if it did not take steps to keep games such as *Mortal Kombat* out of the hands of children.

BONUS POINTS

PS

There is a lot of concern about the effects of screen time on children and teens. The American Academy of Pediatrics recommends that children under two have no screen time and people over two limit their on-screen entertainment. That doesn't include time spent doing educational things, such as writing code! You can read more about some of the issues here.

New York Times screen addiction 🔍

This wasn't the first time that grown-ups had complained about kids' entertainment.

In the 1950s, comic books were considered a bad influence on children. Faced with a crackdown by government officials, comic book publishers set up the Comics Code Authority to decide which comics were safe for kids. This kept the public and the government happy, but many popular comic book companies went out of business.

To avoid government interference, in 1994 the top video game companies created the Entertainment **Software** Rating Board (ESRB). The ESRB created ratings to tell parents which games were safe for specific ages. Games are now labeled.

Games are not required to have ratings, but many stores won't carry a game without one. Today, most stores will not sell an M-rated game, such as *Mortal Kombat*, to anyone under 17 without a parent's approval.

BONUS POINTS

In 1968, the Motion Picture Association of America Inc. also created its own rating system for movies. Movie theaters began using letter codes (G, PG, PG-13, and R) to tell parents whether or not a film was suitable for kids.

THE ESRB RATINGS

EC = Early Childhood: For young children.

E = Everyone: Suitable for all ages.

E10+ = Everyone 10 and Up: May contain mild cartoon violence. Ages 10+.

T = Teen: May contain violence, crude humor and some strong language. Suitable for ages 13+.

M = Mature: May contain intense violence, sexual content, and strong language. Suitable for ages 17+.

AO = Adults Only: May contain intense violence, graphic sexual content, and gambling with real money. For ages 18+.

RP = Rating Pending: Used in promotional materials before a game is assigned a rating.

VIDEO GAMES AND THE POWER OF STORY

If you're a video game fan, you know that games matter to the people who play them. But are they important to the rest of society, too? In 2010, the late film critic Roger Ebert famously declared, "Video games can never be art." He meant that books and movies tell stories that affect the way people view the world, but in video games, it's the players who decide what happens.

Can a video game leave its "audience" with a powerful message if the action is different every time the game is played?

Many people believe that **narrative** games can rise to the level of art, just like books and movies. They point out that games can share many things with movies, including interesting characters, exciting conflict, exotic locations, amazing special effects, and music.

Early games such as *The Legend of Zelda* even used the same structure as classic stories—a hero meets some misfortune and takes ever-increasing risks to try to right it. Most games still use cut scenes, which are short animations between levels that advance the **plot**. But more and more game designers are working to make the story part of the gameplay as well.

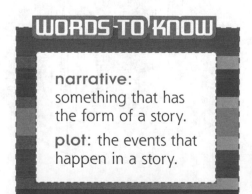

WORDS TO KNOW

narrative: something that has the form of a story.

plot: the events that happen in a story.

Ordinary shooting games or platform jumpers are much more interesting when there are good stories behind the action. For instance, the game *Portal* is a first-person shooter game in the form of a puzzle. The player follows a path through a series of rooms, using a ray gun to blast openings that twist through space and drop the player on a wall or ceiling. The story behind *Portal* involves a prisoner trapped in a futuristic laboratory who must pass a series of tests given by a wily computer named GLaDOS. The computer taunts the player with promises of escape and cake.

Story-driven games are becoming so popular that even *Minecraft*'s maker, Mojang, joined up with Telltale Games to create *Minecraft: Story Mode*.

Maybe the best argument in favor of video games as art form is that they can affect your emotions. Players care about their favorite characters. Games even inspire audiences to get creative themselves.

THE SUPREME COURT SAYS

The **Supreme Court of the United States** has ruled that video games have the same value as other forms of storytelling. In 2011, the court struck down a California law that banned the sale of violent video games to kids, blocking the government from trying to control what video games were about. "Like books, plays and movies, video games communicate ideas," wrote Justice Antonin Scalia. He added that the United States has no laws about other kinds of children's entertainment, pointing out that *Grimm's Fairy Tales*, for example, are grim indeed."

They make videos about the cool things they build on *Minecraft*, create their own *Angry Birds* **fan art**, and **cosplay** as Mario and Luigi. Games tell stories that players want to be a part of. Good storytelling is a powerful way to get players hooked on a game.

Now that you know a little more about the things that make a game popular, it's time to start creating a game of your own. In the next chapter, you'll learn about the steps that go into turning an idea into a game.

Supreme Court of the United States: the highest court in the country, which reviews laws and decisions of lower courts.

fan art: artwork made by a fan of a game, movie, comic book, etc.

cosplay: dressing up in the costume of a character from a video game, movie, etc., for a special event.

WORDS TO KNOW

? ESSENTIAL QUESTION

Now it's time to consider and discuss the Essential Question: How does a video game make you want to keep playing?

GAMIFY AN EVERYDAY CHALLENGE

In 2010, game designer Jane McGonigal created a game called *SuperBetter* to help herself recover from a brain injury. Today, more than 400,000 people have been helped by playing the game. When you sign up on the *SuperBetter* website (superbetter.com) or use the app, you pick a personal goal you're trying to reach, called an "epic win."

The website recommends daily **quests**, which are small steps on the road to meeting your challenge. When you need encouragement, it provides a list of **power-ups** to help you feel better. It also alerts you to "bad guys" that might get in your way. Each time you complete a quest, activate a power-up, or battle a bad guy, it gets added to your progress bar. Try some of these techniques to take a challenge in your life and gamify it.

1 Pick a goal to gamify. It can be a task that's hard to get started on, such as keeping your room neat, or a goal you'd like to reach, such as doing 20 sit-ups. This goal is your Epic Win. Set an amount of time you will play the game, such as a week or a month.

2 Divide your challenge into smaller quests. For instance, if your goal is to keep your room neat, write up a list all the things that need to be done on a regular basis—making your bed, picking up your clothes, straightening your desk, vacuuming the floor. If your Epic Win is to increase your sit-up total, start with five sit-ups and add smaller goals of 10 and 15.

3 Identify some obstacles that might get in the way of your success. These are your bad guys! Find ways to defeat them! If you often forget to do your sit-ups, paste a note on your bedroom mirror to remind yourself. If TV is sucking up time you need to work on your goal, set a limit on how much time you spend in front of the tube.

WORDS TO KNOW

quest: a search or challenge a player must complete to level-up or win a game.

power-up: an object that gives a character more ability or strength.

4 Make a list of power-ups that can give you a quick boost of energy or lift your mood when you need it. This might include drinking a glass of water, taking a walk around the block, or listening to music.

5 Remember, feedback is important. Draw a "progress bar" on a strip of paper and hang it up where you'll see it every day. Divide it into sections equal to the number of your quests. Every time you complete a quest, use a power-up, or conquer a bad guy, color in a section on your progress bar.

6 If you want to add a multiplayer mode, ask your friends and family to join you. They can work on their own goals while helping you with yours. For example, you can make badges or collect some small rewards and give them out at unexpected moments when the challenge is going well.

7 After your gamification experiment is done, go over your notes to see what worked (and what didn't). Did you pick the right power-ups? Did some unexpected bad guys get in your way? Write down your findings, and use them to help you next time you have a goal to meet.

THINK ABOUT IT: What rewards would motivate you to reach your goal faster?

MOD A GAME TO MAKE IT HARDER

Do you remember learning to play tic-tac-toe? The first time you tried it was probably difficult! But it didn't take you long to figure out a few key moves that would let you win—or at least tie. You can **mod** a game to increase the difficulty and bring it up to an achievable challenge. In this activity, you'll mod a non-electronic game to make it harder.

1 Choose a game that's become boring for you and think about ways you can make it harder. The following ideas might help.

- Make the game board bigger.
- Set a timer for each round.
- Create more obstacles, such as spaces that make a player go back to the beginning.

2 Try out your new version of the game and take notes on what works and what doesn't. Is your game still too easy or is it now too hard? Is the harder version more fun or is it just frustrating?

3 Come up with ways to make the game harder for some players but not others so that beginners and experts can play together.

TIC-TAC-TOES!

WORDS TO KNOW

mod: to modify a game to create new levels, characters, or objects— or make a new version—when done by a fan rather than a company.

CHAPTER 3

Gamemaking Step by Step

MOBILE
FUN
ANIMALS
COLORFUL
VIKING
NINJA
KNIGHTS
(or Dragons)

MOUSE
LOBSTER
CATS
DOGS
?

RAT RACE
LEIF QUEST
Dragon Den

PUZZLE
CHASE/RACE
PET SIM
TOWER Defense
PLATFORMER
TRIVIA

Whether you're a big game company, an indie game developer, a college student majoring in game design, or a kid just starting out, the steps involved in creating a new video game are pretty much the same. From developing the first idea and designing the look of the game to testing the finished product, building a game requires many different skills.

In a large company, you might have teams that specialize in one particular part of game development, such as just the characters or just the levels. Hundreds of people might work on one game! In smaller companies, some of the team members may do multiple jobs. One person might design the look of the objects and write the computer programs to make those objects move.

? ESSENTIAL QUESTION

Why do designers need to think logically about the games they are designing?

game assets: any part of the game that the player can see or interact with directly, including characters, objects, backgrounds, text, sound, and special effects.

WORDS TO KNOW

The process for designing a game is very similar for both large and small companies. First, the team brainstorms ideas. Then, they write up the game plans. The team gets feedback from other people and makes changes to the plans.

Designers and developers work on every part of the game, including the **game assets**, the challenges on each level, and the computer programming needed to make it all happen. The entire process can take several months!

Lots of people test the video game and make lots of changes to make sure the game is as perfect as possible before it's sent out into the world.

FINDING THE FUN

Club Penguin, the biggest MMO game for kids, was created in a basement in Canada! Game designer Lance Priebe (who also made *Mancala Snails*) originally made *Club Penguin* in his spare time for his own kids to play. In 2007, Disney bought *Club Penguin* for $700 million. Priebe worked for Disney Interactive until 2009.

Today, he runs Hyper Hippo Games. The first question he asks of any new game is, "Can we find the fun and can we find it fast?" Anyone in the company can propose a game, but they only get two weeks to create a working **prototype**. Priebe prefers starting the design process by building a board game version because, he says, "I get to touch the rules." His board is drawn in the form of a map, he uses action figures as characters, and he makes the buildings and landscape out of Lego pieces.

Once the video game version is ready to test, it's made available on their website. "You don't know what your core feature will be until you put it in front of an audience," Priebe says. "You don't know what game you're designing." Priebe's goal is always a game so good players don't even think about how it works. They just enjoy playing it! You can test out games yourself.

Hyper Hippo 🔍

MAKE YOUR OWN GAME

Even as a beginner, you can follow the same process professionals use to develop your own games: Find an idea, design the look, create a sample, write a plan, build the game, and test the game. Let's take a closer look at these steps.

Find an idea: Game designers look for new ideas in lots of different places. These include other kinds of games, other video games, myths, legends, classic adventure tales, historical events, and game jams. Once you have some ideas to start with, brainstorm!

Can you mash up two different themes and come up with something unique? Can you find a new way to tell a familiar story? Jot down all your ideas. Then decide which one you want to work on.

Design the look: When you've decided on an idea for your game, start thinking about the details. Think about the characters or playing pieces, the setting or background, the art and music, and the story. You also need to design the **gameplay**. Decide on the goal of the game and start coming up with obstacles and rewards that will make the game fun and challenging.

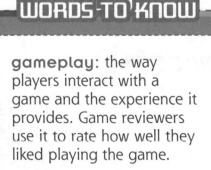

WORDS TO KNOW

gameplay: the way players interact with a game and the experience it provides. Game reviewers use it to rate how well they liked playing the game.

treatment: a short description of how the game works.

Write all these details down in a **treatment**, which is a short, one-page description of the game. Don't worry if you're not sure about any of your decisions. You can always change them later!

GAME TREATMENT CHECKLIST

Your game treatment will help you keep track of what works and what needs to be improved. It should include the following parts.

- ❏ name
- ❏ what the game is about
- ❏ what it looks like, including the style of the cards, the board, and the backgrounds

- ❏ the object of the game
- ❏ the cards, pieces, or characters
- ❏ objects that can help or hurt players along the way
- ❏ how the game is played

Create a sample: It's important to make a quick version of your game to **playtest**. A low-tech run-through lets you know if your idea is good before you invest a lot of time into programming it. At this stage, you only need to think about how it works and if it is fun and interesting to play.

playtest: a research session where players are asked to play an unfinished game while the designers take notes on how it works and players' comments and reactions.

WORDS TO KNOW

Pay attention to whether it's too easy or too frustrating and how long it takes to play a round. Take notes so you remember what you need to work on. Get your friends to test your game, and ask questions to get their opinions on what they like and don't like about it.

BONUS POINTS

When Dejobaan Games made a game about BASE jumping, they wanted to push the limits with a really creative name. They called it *AaaaaAAaaaAAAaaAAAAaAAAAA!!! A Reckless Disregard for Gravity*. This weird title got lots of attention and helped make the game popular!

VIDEO GAMES

design document: a guide for the team that will be working on the game, containing all the details and plans.

reskin: adding new graphics and other design elements to the structure underneath an existing game.

WORDS TO KNOW

Do you and your friends enjoy the game? Is it both interesting and entertaining? If so, it's worth developing more!

Don't worry if the game doesn't work. Try changing one piece of the game at a time to see if you can fix it. If you can't, set it aside and try something different.

Write a plan: Now it's time to create a detailed **design document**. The design document is like a movie script or the blueprint of a building. It's the guidebook for every member of your team.

Build the game: If you're making a board or card game, you'll create all the artwork. If it's a video game, you'll do that plus make it work on a computer! Find some volunteers and have them play through one level or round. If your game is designed for younger children who can't read yet, playtest it with a group of preschoolers. If it's an app for grown-ups, ask your parents to give it a try.

MAKE SOMETHING NEW, FAST!

A quick way to make a new game is to **reskin** an existing game. You can change the entire gameplay by changing the look, objects, or characters. The free puzzle game *2048*, in which players slide numbered tiles around to make them double up, was a reskin of a mobile game called *Threes*. Many fans of the free version never realized is was a reskin of an earlier game! You'll reskin a game in Chapter 5.

DESIGN DOCUMENT CHECKLIST

A design document has much more detail than a treatment. Here are some of the sections included.

❑ **Vision:** What kind of a game is this—adventure, puzzle, edutainment? Is it cartoony, supernatural, realistic history? Who will want to play it? How is it like other games and how is it different?

❑ **Gameplay:** Using your prototype as a guide, describe how the game is played. What is the goal? How do players progress through the game? What are the rules?

❑ **Story:** If your game has a story, write a summary that follows the same order that players will discover it. Write a script that tells what happens and what the characters say. Include instructions, background information from the narrator, and conversations between the different characters.

❑ **Gameworld:** Your document should describe where your game is set and what each level looks like. You will also need to draw maps of each level.

❑ **Characters:** Describe your main characters, the enemies they face, and any other characters they meet throughout the game. Characters can be divided into **playable characters (PC)** and **non-playable characters (NPC)**. NPCs can be helpers or enemies or **bosses** that the player must defeat to move on. They might also be neutral characters that just hang around. For all characters, decide how they look and sound, how they move, their strengths and weaknesses, and any special abilities.

playable characters (PC): characters or avatars in a video game that are controlled by the players.

non-playable characters (NPC): characters in a video game that are controlled by the computer program, not including enemies.

bosses: the main enemy in one level of a game that must be defeated to move on.

WORDS TO KNOW

BONUS POINTS

Chris Egert of the Rochester Institute of Technology's Center for Media, Arts, Games, Interaction and Creativity (MAGIC), says you can make a great game from ancient myths or classic science fiction stories. He advises his students to ask themselves, "What sort of worlds can I make with that? How can I take something and twist it around?"

quality assurance (QA): playing a game that is nearly finished to find any problems before it is published.

bug: a mistake in the code that causes unexpected problems.

conditional scripting: the part of a script or plan for a game that shows what happens when a player makes one choice or another.

WORDS TO KNOW

Test the game: The final level of testing is called **quality assurance (QA)**. QA engineers explore every level and test every possible choice a player can make. They are looking for **bugs**. Check to see if there's anyplace your characters can get stuck or walk off the edge. Do some destructive testing to find out if there is anything that will accidentally make your game freeze or crash, such as pushing two buttons at the same time.

According to independent game designer Amy Kraft, "The best QA testers love breaking the game."

BONUS POINTS

Gaming companies often ask kids from the community to come to their studios and playtest new games. If you're one of the volunteers chosen to help make a new game better, you might find your name in the game's credits when it comes out!

If your game tells a story, check the **conditional scripting** to see if your game does what you want it to do. If not, go back to the beginning, fix the problems, and go through all the testing steps again.

CHEAT CODES

Cheat codes are "secret" keyboard or controller **commands** that let you jump a level, make you invincible, or give you an unlimited number of lives. The first cheats were the result of a bug in the programming or a backdoor built in by **programmers** to help them move through the game quickly as they built and tested it. Later, those cheat code bugs became features that every player could use, if they could figure out the commands!

The QA process can be used whenever you build something new, whether it's a video game or robot, to make it as good a design as possible! Now that you know the basics of game design, you can learn how to code your game into a video game.

SAMPLE GAME TREATMENT

The sample game treatment on the following spread shows you how you might turn *Goldilocks and the Three Bears* into a game. The map helps you plan the action.

cheat codes: keyboard commands that let you skip steps or give you extra powers.

command: an instruction in the form of code that tells a computer to do something. Also called a statement.

programmer: a person who writes computer programs. Also called a coder.

How would you have written the treatment differently? Is there anything else that you think should be included?

What it's about: *Goldilocks and the Three Bears* is a text adventure comedy game for one player about a lost little girl named Goldilocks. She finds a house in the woods belonging to three bears. The game is aimed at younger children.

Goal: Goldilocks (the player) must collect objects from the bears' house to survive in the woods. She must escape before they return from their walk.

Characters:

- Goldilocks, an adventurous little girl with golden hair

- Papa Bear, a large, fierce animal with scruffy fur, long claws, and large teeth

- Mama Bear, a medium-sized animal with perfectly combed fur and a slightly angry expression

- Baby Bear, a cute cub with big eyes and a friendly expression

Setting: The game takes place in a little cottage deep in the woods, surrounded by trees. Because the owners are bears, the cottage feels like a cave. The cottage has a kitchen and living room on the first floor, and a bedroom upstairs under the eaves.

There are three exits—a heavy wooden front door, a staircase in the living room leading to the second floor, and a small, round bedroom window just big enough for Goldilocks to fit through.

BONUS POINTS

The British Council created a video game from the story of Goldilocks to help kids learn to speak English. You can play it here.

Porridge Puzzle 🔍

Objects:

- The kitchen has a rough wooden table with three chairs. On it are three bowls of porridge. One bowl is frozen solid. One will release a plume of steam when a spoon is inserted. The third just sits there.

- In the living room there are three identical chairs. One is solid, another folds up, and the third is easily breakable.

- In the bedroom there are three identical blankets.

Gameplay: The player must collect an object from each room and avoid the bears as she moves though the house: a bowl, a chair that folds so it can be carried, and a blanket big enough to keep her warm but not too big to carry. As she searches, the bears come home and look around to see what has happened. If the bears catch Goldilocks, she drops the objects she has already collected and is chased out of the house. If she collects all the objects and escapes before the bears catch her, the player wins. Players can adjust the timer to make the game easier or harder.

Challenges: The player must figure out which identical bowl of porridge isn't too hot or too cold, which chair will fold up, and which blanket is just right—without falling asleep on the bed.

Bonuses: The player can earn extra time before the bears find her by straightening up each room before she leaves.

? ESSENTIAL QUESTION

Now it's time to consider and discuss the Essential Question: Why do designers need to think logically about the games they are designing?

PLAYTEST AN EXISTING GAME

IDEAS FOR SUPPLIES
board game that is new to you

**Learn to improve games by thinking about
them as you play or watch others play.**

1 Write down the name of the game and the company that made it
on a page in your notebook. Also write down the date and who will be
playing it. Divide the paper in half by making a 2-column chart like the
one below. Mark one half *Like* and the other half *Don't Like*.

LIKE	DON'T LIKE

2 As you play, write down whatever you and your friends like or don't
like. Try to find four or five positive and negative things about the game.

3 When you're done playing, write down ideas for fixing the things you didn't like. For example, if it's a card game that you found too easy, try adding more cards to each player's hand to make it tougher. If it's a board game with dice, try adding a rule that anyone who rolls a double loses a turn.

4 Now try another **iteration** by repeating Steps 2 and 3, changing one rule at a time. Continue to take notes about what works and what doesn't until you are happy with the result.

A CLASS CREATES A GAME

Game designer Amy Kraft of Monkey Bar Collective in New York City helped her daughter's first-grade class create its own card game based on its favorite science topic—animals. Their idea was to combine the concept of a food chain with math. The class researched the food chain for details about which animals eat which other animals.

Then they needed to come up with some rules. How many cards would there be? How many points would each card be worth? Usually game designers need to balance the system to make sure one element alone doesn't make a player sure to win. In this game, the students had to make the cards add up to certain numbers. For instance, the numbers of two fish cards had to equal the number on the card of a fish-eating animal. Then the playtesting began. Some students played, while others watched and took notes. They kept refining the rules until everything worked.

They also came up with a catchy name—*Animal Food Fight.* When the game was finished, the students held a launch party to celebrate their achievement.

CREATE A FOUND-OBJECT GAME BOARD

IDEAS FOR SUPPLIES

large pieces of paper ❖ *dice, game spinner, blank cards, or cut-up pieces of paper* ❖ *recycled materials such as buttons, bottle caps, old dolls, minifigs, or action figures* ❖ *cardstock or cardboard*

Mix it up! Start with a new kind of board and see what games it inspires.

1 Sketch a rough outline of a game board using any design you like. You can make a grid like a checkerboard or *Scrabble* board, a wavy path like the one in *Candy Land* or *Chutes and Ladders*, or a square of spaces as in *Monopoly*.

2 Gather some recycled materials to use as game pieces. Using your board and pieces for inspiration, brainstorm ideas for a new game. Write down as many ideas as you can in 15 minutes—the crazier the better! It doesn't matter whether they will work or not. Brainstorming is for coming up with lots of new and interesting ideas.

3 Look through your ideas for some that seem possible. You may want to try combining ideas. Choose the best idea and write it up as a very short game treatment. Check the list in the chapter for what to include in the treatment.

4 Make any additions to the board that might be needed to help players figure out what to do, such as colors, labels, or directions. This is just your prototype, so don't worry if it's messy! You'll make a better version later. If you need dice or a spinner, you can borrow them from a game you own.

5 Playtest your game, using the process described above. Make any changes needed and try it again.

6 When you have a working prototype, make a nicer board using stiff cardboard and colorful art materials. Keep playing and refining your game. Keep track of new rules and other changes as you make them.

BONUS POINTS

Have you ever played with a Rubik's Cube? Erno Rubik, an architect, invented it by accident. He was trying to create a cube with parts that could twist and turn without coming apart. After putting colorful stickers on his cube, he demonstrated how it moved, and then it took him a month to solve his own puzzle! You can try an online version here.

kp rubik's cube online 🔍

DESIGN A MEMORY CARD GAME

IDEAS FOR SUPPLIES
identical index cards ❖ *art supplies*

Have you ever played *Memory*? That's the game where you start with a set of cards in which every card has one other card that matches it. All the cards look the same from the back. You lay the cards out face down in a grid and turn them over two at a time, trying to find a match. You win by matching up the most pairs of cards. In this activity, you will design, prototype, and test your own variation on this classic memory game.

1 Brainstorm some ideas for a new kind of matching card game.

Here are some ideas to get you started, then come up with more of your own.

- Create a code that equates one object with another.
  For example, a green circle is equal to the word "elephant."
  Players get two minutes to memorize the code. Instead of matching two cards that each show a green circle, players match each image to its code word or symbol.

- For each pair of cards you turn over, you might be able to match it in three different areas, such as color, shape, and size of objects. Every area of match gets a point. For instance, a big blue square and a little red square would be worth one point. A little blue square and a little blue circle would be worth two points. The player may choose whether to accept those two cards as a match, or put them back and try for a better match.

- Turn it into a game for two or more players, with one player acting as judge for each round. Using cards with no matches, make each player explain to the judge why their pair should be considered a match.

2 Pick one idea and make a prototype with rough drawings sketched on the index cards. A good number of cards to play with for each round is 16. Your version of the game might use more cards or a different number of cards in each round.

3 Playtest your game. What can you do to improve it? Make changes and try again.

4 When you're satisfied, create a final set of cards. If you don't want to draw the final designs on the cards by hand, you can print pictures off the Internet or cut them out from old magazines. Just be sure the images don't show through from the back. If they do, glue a second blank card to the back to make them thicker.

TRY THIS: You can create a family photo memory game by using pictures of your family! Ask a parent to help you go through your family photo albums and pick out pictures from each of your family members. Include pictures of your family pets and those old black-and-white photos of when your grandparents were little. Be sure to make copies of the photos you choose so that the originals stay intact.

BONUS POINTS

House rules are ways to play a game that make it easier, harder, or more fun in some way. A popular house rule for *Monopoly* is to give all the fines paid during the game to a player who lands on Free Parking. Does your family play this way?

WRITE A GAME TREATMENT

Choose a favorite story and turn it into a text-based adventure game, then write up a treatment for it.

1 Pick a story to use as the basis of a game. You can choose a fairy tale, your favorite book, or a story you've written yourself.

2 Write the story down in the form of a game treatment. Use the Sample Game Treatment for a Goldilocks Text Adventure as a model. Although your text adventure will not include images, be sure to describe the places, objects, and characters so players can create pictures in their own minds.

3 A text adventure usually involves exploring a space with different rooms or areas, so draw a map of the game area. Mark all the objects and characters on it. This is just for planning purposes, so don't worry about making it perfect.

THINK ABOUT IT: In the next chapter, you'll learn how to turn your idea into instructions the computer can read and understand! If you'd like to try your hand at creating a playable version instantly, websites such as Twine and Text Adventures are free programs that let you enter in your information and create a game in minutes!

Twine or Text Adventures 🔍

CHAPTER 4

Coding: How to Write a Game Program

Everything in a video game comes from the gamemaker's imagination, including how characters act, how objects move, and every twist and turn of the storyline. How does the game get from your brain to your screen? It must be translated into a list of instructions your computer can understand—a computer program.

The people who write, or code, computer programs are called programmers or coders. To build games, they use **programming languages** such as Java, Python, or C++. Each language has its own set of commands or statements, which are similar to the words in a spoken language.

WORDS TO KNOW

programming language: a language invented to communicate instructions to a computer.

? ESSENTIAL QUESTION

How is programming a computer game like baking cookies?

VIDEO GAMES

Computer languages also have their own **syntax**, which is like the grammar you use to put words together into a sentence. Syntax includes what order the commands go in and what punctuation marks are used. For example, in English you generally end a sentence with a period. In Java every line of code must end with a semicolon (;) or the computer won't read the code correctly.

Some programming languages are better for certain things, so programmers often learn more than one. Mastering a new language can take time, because every letter, symbol, and space must be exactly right.

Luckily, there are tools designed to help beginners start coding without having to learn to write an entirely new language!

Visual programming languages (VPL) such as Scratch, Tynker, and Blockly let you build programs using **drag-and-drop** blocks instead of typing in commands. You simply use your computer mouse to move the block you want to the right spot. The blocks snap together to form a column on your screen, and you read your program from top to bottom. Other kinds of game programming environments include Unity, Construct 2, Stencyl, and GameMaker Studio.

BONUS POINTS

The number system you use every day has 10 digits: 0, 1, 2, 3, 4, 5, 6, 7, 8, and 9. It is known as a Base 10 number system.

COMPUTER TALK

Computers are machines, and they understand **machine language**. They are made up of billions of electronic switches called **transistors** that are either turned off or on. Machine language is made up of only two numbers: zero for off, and one for on. This number system is called **binary**.

machine language: the code used directly by a computer, written in zeroes and ones.

transistor: a small device that acts as an on/off switch to control the flow of electricity in a computer.

binary: a math system containing only zeroes and ones. The word binary comes from the Latin word *bi* for "two," as in bicycle and binoculars.

bit: the basic unit of information storage in a computer, consisting of a zero or a one.

byte: a group of eight bits that is treated as a single piece of information.

WORDS TO KNOW

Each zero and each one is also known as a binary digit, or **bit**. Machine language groups those bits into groups of eight to form a **byte**. A byte can be used to represent a letter, number, or symbol. In machine language, the word "hello" is written like this:

H	E	L	L	O
01101000	01100101	01101100	01101100	01101111

All computer programs, no matter how advanced, are really nothing but zeroes and ones!

VIDEO GAMES

algorithm: a series of steps to complete a task. There can be different algorithms to do the same thing.

sequence of commands: the order of the steps in a program.

function: a short piece of code that is given a name so it can be used multiple times in a program simply by inserting the name. Also called a subroutine or procedure.

loop: a section of code that is repeated a certain number of times or until a specific condition is met.

WORDS TO KNOW

THINK LIKE A PROGRAMMER

The most important thing you need to learn before coding isn't how to write any particular language, it's how to break down a problem or action into a series of steps. This series of steps is called an **algorithm**.

Think of an algorithm as a recipe for baking a computer program.

When you make chocolate chip cookies, your recipe tells you all the things you'll need to do. Of course, the **sequence of commands** is also important. If you don't follow the steps in the right order, your cookies—or your program—might not come out the way you expect!

Looking at problems as a series of steps can also help you find patterns that repeat over and over. And computers are good at repeating patterns. That means you don't have to write out each step every time, which makes programming easier and faster! There are two main ways to do this: **functions** and **loops**.

BONUS POINTS

In 2013, Google executive Dan Shapiro invented a board game called *Robot Turtles* to teach coding basics to young children. The game shows kids how to break big problems into small steps as they move their turtles through a maze. The game became an overnight hit, selling 25,000 copies before it was even printed.

A function is an algorithm that is given its own name. Instead of writing out all the steps, you just write the name instead.

For example, in the Goldilocks text adventure game from the previous chapter, the little girl finds three bowls of porridge and performs the same series of steps for each one.

You can **define a function** called *tasting* to perform these tasks.

• Sit down at the table.

• Pick up the spoon next to a bowl.

• Dip it into the bowl.

• Put the spoonful of porridge in her mouth and swallow.

define a function: to tell the computer what steps a function contains.

call a function: to tell the computer program to run a function.

variable: a symbol that holds the place for information that may change each time a command runs.

data: information, usually given in the form of numbers, that can be processed by a computer.

string: a short group of letters or words that is used as data.

WORDS TO KNOW

`<tasting>`

Each time Goldilocks comes upon a new bowl, you can just **call the function** *tasting* and the program will repeat those steps.

You can also insert **variables** into your function. This is a letter or word that can be replaced with different information. The information must be in the form of **data** that can be processed by a computer. It can consist of numbers or a **string** of letters that make up a word or group of words. When you run the program, the variable tells it to look for the information in another part of the program or asks the player to fill it in.

A loop is a little like a function. But instead of running whenever you call its name, a loop keeps repeating as many times as you tell it to.

Another way to tell a loop to stop is to use conditional statements.

These tell a program to check whether or not certain conditions exist before continuing.

One common conditional statement is **IF-THEN-ELSE.** For example, IF the porridge is just right, THEN Goldilocks will eat it.

A **WHILE statement** tells the program to check to see if the condition is still true. WHILE the porridge is cooling, the bears will continue their walk. Every time they return to their house, they check the porridge to see if they should keep walking.

Conditional statements are a type of **Boolean logic.** Because a computer can only understand "on" and "off," Boolean logic reduces every decision to two possible choices: True or False.

You can also expand the conditions using three **logic gates:** NOT (the condition is not true), AND (there are two conditions and both are true), and OR (there are two conditions and at least one of them is true).

You could say that if the bears are still on their walk AND the porridge is NOT too hot OR too cold, THEN Goldilocks will eat it.

BEFORE YOU CODE

Planning your computer program can help you code it correctly and make it easier to find problems when you test it. Here are a few best practices to try.

Write it out. Before you translate your game into a computer language, list all the steps using **pseudocode**. Write down all the actions you want your program to perform. Later, you can translate it into whichever programming language you decide to use.

TIC-TAC-TOE PSEUDOCODE

Here is one way to write out pseudocode for a game of tic-tac-toe. Notice that there are three different ways the game program can end.

- ❏ WHILE there are empty squares on the tic-tac-toe board

- ❏ Player 1 puts an X in a square.

- ❏ IF there are three Xs in a row, THEN Player 1 wins.

- ❏ ELSE Player 2 puts an O in one of the squares.

- ❏ IF there are three Os in a row, THEN Player 2 wins.

- ❏ ELSE REPEAT from Player 1's turn

- ❏ GAME ENDS in a tie (no winner).

WORDS TO KNOW

pseudocode: from the Greek word for false, this is an algorithm written in language a human can read and understand.

69

Draw a flowchart. A **flowchart** is a diagram that shows all your possible options and the results for each one. These options can be shown as Yes/No or True/False statements. Flowcharts are also helpful for showing how loops work.

Organize it with a chart. A chart can be a great help in keeping track of all the objects and characters in your game. Your chart should have three columns.

- **Name and category:** these are the objects and characters.

- **Properties:** what it looks like, how many versions are needed, where and when it starts.

- **Actions and abilities:** any movement or changes in appearance, any interaction with other objects or characters.

BONUS POINTS

An old saying from the early days of computers is, "Garbage In, Garbage Out" or GIGO. It means a computer is only as accurate as its programs. As a programmer, you need to test your code for syntax bugs, which are mistakes caused by typing errors, and logical bugs, which are problems putting the right steps in the right order. Test your coding just like you test every other part of your game.

Goldilocks Flowchart

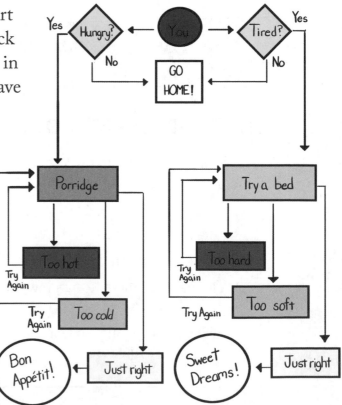

GOLDILOCKS GAME CHART

Here is a sample game chart showing objects and characters in the Goldilocks game.

Name and Category	Properties	Actions and Abilities
Goldilocks (PC)	Little girl; curious, happy, and scared expressions	Goes into each room and pokes into whatever objects it contains
Papa Bear (boss)	Big and fierce	Goes for walk in woods; chases Goldilocks out of house
Mama Bear (NPC)	Medium sized and fussy	Goes for walk in woods; annoyed when house is messy
Baby Bear (NPC)	Small and full of mischief	Goes for walk in woods; surprises sleeping Goldilocks
The Three Bears' Cottage (background)	Cozy and cute; contains kitchen, living room, and bedroom	Doors and window open and close
Bowl of porridge (object)	Two versions, full and empty	Goldilocks must eat all the porridge to leave the kitchen

CODING IN SCRATCH

Scratch is a great first programming language to learn. It was developed for kids in 2003 by computer scientist Mitch Resnick and the Scratch Team at the Lifelong Kindergarten group. This group is part of the Massachusetts Institute of Technology Media Lab.

What makes Scratch special is the online community where you can share your work. You can get feedback on your projects and learn from projects that other Scratch members have done.

The Scratch site is moderated, so it's safe for kids to use at school or at home.

One way Scratch helps you learn to code is with the "See Inside" feature, which shows you the programming for any project on the site. You are also encouraged to "remix" other people's projects, which is when you make a copy for yourself that you can then change to create your own version. The rules on the Scratch website allow anyone to remix any of the projects found there.

Getting started is easy. Go to the Scratch website at scratch.mit.edu and start creating programs right away. When you create a free account, you can save your work and share it with others. You can also download Scratch to your computer's hard drive so you can use it without having to connect to the Internet.

BONUS POINTS

One of the first programs ever written by Microsoft founder Bill Gates was an algorithm to make the computer play tic-tac-toe.

DOCUMENTATION

If you look at code written in programming languages such as Python and Java, you might notice short notes in English that tell you what is going on. This **documentation** is a powerful tool for helping programmers fix problems in their code. You should always document the programs you write so you or another programmer knows what each step is supposed to do. In many languages, a double slash (//) is inserted before any documentation comments. That tells the computer to ignore whatever comes next on that line. For human brains only!

WORDS TO KNOW

documentation: an explanation of a section of computer code, written in non-machine language.

The Scratch projects in this book were built using Scratch 2.0. If you are using a computer with an earlier version, the look of the workspace and some of the features will be a little different.

You can start a new Scratch project by clicking *Create* at the top of the screen. This will take you to the **user interface (UI)**, where you will build your project. Let's look at the different parts of building a program.

user interface (UI): in Scratch, the screen where you build your project.

sprite: an object or character.

costume: a variation of a sprite that looks somewhat different from the original.

stage: the background of a Scratch project.

WORDS TO KNOW

Sprites and costumes: When you open Scratch, you'll already have a character there to play with—the Scratch Cat. In Scratch, objects and characters, such as the Scratch Cat, are known as **sprites**.

All the sprites you use in your project are displayed in the lower left section of the screen, the Sprite List.

You can add other sprites from the library on the Scratch website. Just click on the menu bar above the Sprite List.

To change the look of a sprite during a game, you can add a **costume**. In Scratch, a costume doesn't refer to clothes. It's an image of the same character, but in a different position. For instance, to make an animation of the Scratch Cat walking, you can add several costumes with its legs in different positions and switch between them quickly. There is also a Sprite Toolbar above the **stage** with buttons that let you duplicate, delete, grow, and shrink them.

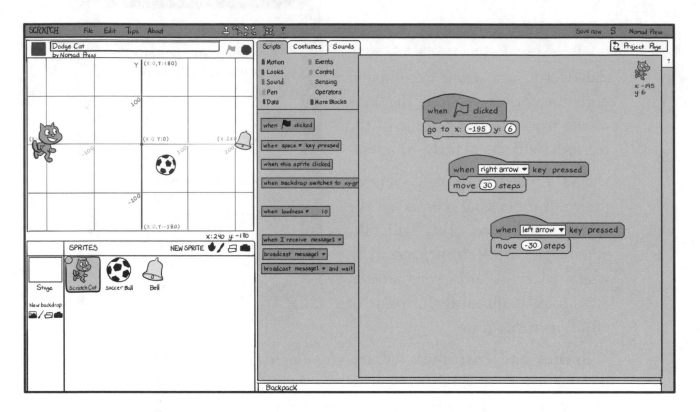

Stage and backdrops: The Scratch Cat and other sprites do all their activities on a large space called the stage. This is a small version of what a player sees on the screen when your program runs.

> When you're programming, the stage lets you see immediately what happens when you add, take away, or change things.

Backdrops are backgrounds for the stage. On the left edge of the Sprite List, you'll see a column with a thumbnail of the current backdrop in your project. Click on that column to open the Backdrops Tab. Here you can choose a new backdrop from the library or create your own. Backdrops can also be programmed to interact with the characters, objects, or users.

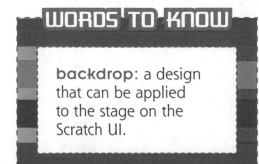

WORDS TO KNOW

backdrop: a design that can be applied to the stage on the Scratch UI.

Stage coordinates: Scratch uses **geometry** to help your sprites find their way around the stage. One helpful backdrop, the xy grid, divides the stage using a system of crossed lines. The **horizontal** line that passes through the middle of the stage is the **x-axis**.

```
Dodge Cat
by Nomad Press
```

Y (X:0,Y:180)

100

(X:_ _)   (X:0,Y:0)   (X:240)

-100   100   200

100

-100

(X:0,Y:-180)

x:240, y:-180

The x-axis is similar to a number line because there is a zero at the center and it counts to 240 on the right and to -240 on the left. The **vertical** line that passes through the middle of the stage is the **y-axis**. It's numbers go to 180 at the top and -180 at the bottom.

Every point on the stage where these lines cross can be identified by a pair of numbers. The first number shows where it is along the x-axis and the second number shows where it is along the y-axis. These numbers are called the **xy coordinates**.

geometry: a branch of mathematics that deals with points, lines, and shapes and where they are in space.

horizontal: going straight across from side to side.

x-axis: the horizontal line on a graph that passes through the center point (0,0). Points are measured by how far to the left or right of the y-axis they are.

vertical: going straight up and down.

y-axis: the vertical line on a graph that passes through the center point (0,0). Points are measured by how far above or below the x-axis they are.

xy coordinates: a pair of numbers written like this (x,y) that tell where a point is on a graph, measured from the x-axis and y-axis.

WORDS TO KNOW

For example, the center of the stage is shown as (0,0). Move three lines to the right and two lines down and you are at (3,-2). You can always see the coordinates of any spot on the stage by placing your mouse over it and reading the x and y numbers shown at the bottom right of the stage. The grid helps you plan out the movements of your sprites.

Sprite coordinates: Sprites have their own personal coordinates that move around with them. When you first place a sprite on the stage and tell a sprite to move, it will go forward, meaning left to right, unless told otherwise. To make it move in a different direction, point it in that direction by giving it the coordinates it should face in **degrees**.

To understand how it works, imagine the sprite is in the exact center of a big square. Now imagine a horizontal line and a vertical line to divide the big square into four smaller squares.

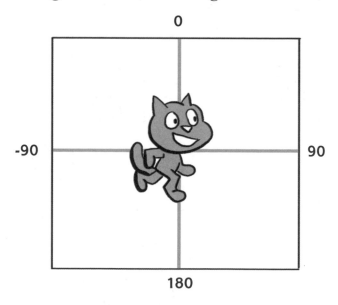

Each corner of a square forms an angle measuring 90 degrees. If 0 points up, 90 degrees points to the right along the edges of the squares to the sprite's right. Directions to the left of the vertical line are indicated by negative numbers. So -90 degrees points to the left. To get the measurement for straight down, you add 90 and 90 to get 180 degrees.

Blocks and scripts: In Scratch, programs are called **scripts,** and they go in the Scripts Area on the right of the screen. All the scripts you write will be connected to either a sprite or a backdrop.

You can even make a blank backdrop or an invisible sprite and still connect code to it.

When you click on a sprite or a backdrop, the programming that goes with it is displayed in the Scripts Area. Scripts are made by creating stacks of blocks. You can find them in the Blocks Palette column between the stage and the Scripts Area.

Blocks are color-coded according to type—Motion, Looks, Sound, Pen, Data, Events, Control, Sensing, and Operators. They also come in different shapes, depending on their use.

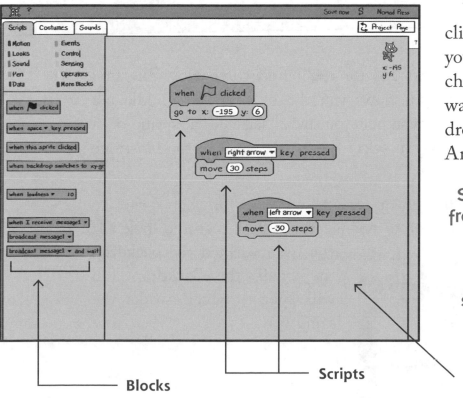

To make a script, click on the category you'd like to use, choose the block you want, and drag-and-drop it into the Scripts Area with your mouse.

Stack the blocks from top to bottom in the order you want them to run. Once stacked, blocks stick together.

Blocks

Scripts

Scripts Area

77

HOW TO CONTROL BLOCKS AND SCRIPTS

- ❑ To remove a block from the script, pull it away from below. Grabbing a stack of blocks from above moves the entire stack.

- ❑ To delete a block, use the scissors icon in the Sprites toolbar or drag it back into the Blocks Palette.

- ❑ Each sprite or background can have several scripts running at the same time. Breaking the programming into smaller chunks makes it easier to write and debug.

- ❑ If you have several separate scripts floating around the space and want to make them neater, right-click in the Scripts Area. A box will pop up that gives you the choice to Clean Up the area.

- ❑ To document your code in Scratch, right-click in the Scripts Area and choose *Comment*. A little yellow box will appear where you can type in some text. Comments make the script run more slowly, so use them only where necessary.

Tabs: Above the Blocks Palette you'll find three tabs. The first is the Scripts Tab, which shows you the blocks. The middle tab changes depending on whether you have selected a sprite or a backdrop **thumbnail**. If you select one of the sprites, the Costume Tab will appear.

Open it to see what costumes are available for that sprite, to choose a new costume, or to change the way a costume looks. If you have selected the backdrop thumbnail, the Backdrop Tab will appear, which works the same way.

WORDS TO KNOW

thumbnail: a small copy of an image on a computer, usually linked to the full-sized version.

The last tab opens up the Sound Palette. That lets you choose a new sound for your sprite or backdrop, and edit the sound you have selected.

Start: To run a Scratch program, you usually click on a green flag. The red stop sign shape ends it. But you can program Scratch to respond to clicks on other objects, different colors, or different sounds. You can also make it respond when a particular key is pressed on the keyboard. You can give players directions for using your game on a backdrop or in the description on the project page. This is the page other people see when they first go to your project.

Help: Scratch offers many ways to find help about all the things you can do with the program. You can see the help menu by clicking on the tiny question mark in the upper right-hand corner. The help menu contains animated guides to help you get started.

Another way to get help is to right-click on any block to bring up information on how it works.

The Scratch Help Page, which can be found at scratch.mit.edu/help, has more links, guides, and video tutorials. You can also go to the Scratch **Wiki**, which can be found at wiki.scratch.mit.edu/wiki. The Scratch Wiki is largely written by Scratch users and is a good place to search when you are looking for answers to specific questions.

? ESSENTIAL QUESTION

Now it's time to consider and discuss the Essential Question: How is programming a computer game like baking cookies?

WORDS TO KNOW

wiki: a free website that allows users to write and edit articles explaining a topic or range of topics.

GAME JAM ACTIVITY

IDEAS FOR SUPPLIES

game you like to play, such as your memory game from Chapter 3

Every game gives players choices to make and steps to follow. A flowchart is a quick way to show how those options lead to different results. In this activity, you will make a drawing that shows how a game works.

A flowchart uses different shapes to indicate different kinds of steps.

- Start and End blocks are oval.

- Diamond-shaped Decision blocks mark where a choice is made. These are usually yes/no or true/false questions.

- Rectangles indicate where an Action will be performed.

Start/End   Decision   Action

1 Draw a flowchart for a game of your choice that starts with the first move. Include all the possible ways players can move through the game, using the correct shapes. Use arrows to show directions. You might be surprised at how many steps even a simple game can take from beginning to end!

BONUS POINTS

Mark Engelberg is the inventor of *Code Master*, a board game that teaches kids programming logic. He says that the one thing everyone should know about coding is that computer programs are made of reusable parts. Functions and loops and the way they can be layered inside one another make programming powerful!

SCRATCH CAT DODGE BALL

IDEAS FOR SUPPLIES
computer with access to Scratch

Video games that involve multiple levels, characters, and objects require a lot of planning. But you can build a quick game using tools such as Scratch. In this activity, you will create a very simple game in which players must dash across the screen and ring the bell without getting hit by the ball. Once you've got the basic tools and commands mastered, you'll be on your way to programming your own video game prototypes!

This game requires three sprites that perform some simple roles. Here's a chart to give you an idea of what they do.

Name and Category	Properties	Actions and Abilities
Scratch Cat (PC)	main character	Can move back and forth across the stage
Soccer Ball	object	Bounces across the screen. If it touches Scratch Cat, game over
Bell	object	Ring it to win the game

1 Open up Scratch and create a new project. Refer back to the chapter for help if you need it. The Scratch Cat sprite is automatically supplied—it will be called Sprite 1. You can change the name by right-clicking on the image in the Sprite List and clicking "Info" in the menu that appears. You will create three scripts.

- One moves the Scratch Cat at the left of the stage when the game starts.

- The other two make it move back and forth.

PROJECT CONTINUES ON NEXT PAGE

81

2 Start by building the Scratch Cat. In the Block Palette, click on the dark brown Events category.

- Drag and drop *when [flag] clicked* to the Scripts Area.
- Drag and drop *when space key pressed* into the Scripts Area. Click on the triangle after the word *space*. Choose right arrow. Repeat with another copy of the same block and set it to left arrow.

Click on the dark blue Motion category.

- Drag the block *go to x: [ ] go to y: [ ]* and snap it to *when [flag] clicked*.
- Under the right arrow block, snap the Motion block that says *move [ ] steps*. Set the number of steps to 30 by clicking in the box. Do the same for the left arrow block, changing the number to -30.

Stop and test your code by clicking on the green flag. Use the arrow keys to move the Scratch Cat. Which way does it go?

3 To code the soccer ball, click on the little creature in the New Sprite toolbar and open the sprite library. Select the soccer ball. You'll need to build three separate sections for the soccer ball script.

- To tell the ball where to be at the start of the game connect the *when [flag] clicked* block and a *x: [ ] go to y: [ ]* motion block as before. Set x to 0 and y to -158.
- To make the sprite move up and down, add a *point in direction* block, click the triangle, and set it to *up*. The number 0 will appear.
- To keep the ball bouncing across the stage, use a loop. Drag a *forever* block from the Controls category into the Scripts Area, separate from the others. To make a loop, insert the following Motion blocks into the opening of the *forever* block: *change x by [ ]* and set it at 1; *move [ ] steps* set to 10; *if on edge, bounce*.

4 To make the ball play a Game Over sound if it touches the Scratch Cat, use a conditional statement.

- From the Control category, drag an *if [ ] then* block. The diamond in the center is where you put your condition.

- From the Sensing category choose the *touching [ ]?* block. Click the little triangle and choose the Scratch Cat sprite name.

- Drag the Sensing block over the diamond in the Control block until the diamond lights up and then snap it into place.

- Drag a *stop [ ]* block into the opening of the *if [ ] then* block and set it to *all*.

- From the Sound category choose *play sound [ ] until done*. The pull-down menu shows any sounds that come with your sprite. Click on the popping sound to select it for that block. The Sound block goes directly above the *stop* block.

5 Connect all the sections of the soccer ball script. Drag the entire *if [ ] then* block into the mouth of the *forever* block and snap it in below the Motion blocks. Snap the entire *forever* block to the bottom of the stack under the *when [flag] clicked* block. Test before moving on.

6 To create the bell, find and add the bell sprite to your project.

- Start with the *when [flag] clicked* Events block.

- Go to the Control blocks and drag over the *wait until [ ]* block.

- Find the *touching [ ]* block in the Sensing category, set it to the Scratch Cat sprite, and snap it into the Control block. Add a *stop [all]* block at the end.

- From the Sounds category, insert a *play sound [ ] until done* block between the Control blocks. It should be set to *bell toll*.

- Test out the bell script alone. If it works, you can test and play the whole game!

WRITE A PSEUDOCODE ALGORITHM

IDEAS FOR SUPPLIES
memory game from Chapter 3

In this activity, you will use ordinary English words instead of a programming language to program a memory game.

1 Demonstrate your game as if you were teaching it to someone else. If your game needs more than one player, you can play for all of them. Make notes about every step as you go. Look for patterns of moves that are repeated throughout the game.

2 Write a complete set of instructions in the form of a pseudocode algorithm. Where the same steps are repeated exactly, you can create a loop or a function.

Sample set of instructions.

- Turn the cards so the blank backs are facing you.
- Mix them up.
- Place them face down in four rows of four cards each in front of you (the playing area).
- While there are still cards in the playing area:
    - Pick one card at random and turn it over;
    - Do the same with a second card.

3 To test your pseudocode, give it to someone who doesn't know how to play your game and ask him or her to follow your instructions. Watch as they try to play to see if you left out any steps or mixed up the order. Make changes as necessary.

WHERE ARE THE GIRLS?

In 2015, 12-year-old Maddie Messer did a study and found that out of the top 50 endless running iPhone apps with human characters, 98 percent offered boy characters, but only 46 percent had any girl characters at all. And while 90 percent of those games had free boy characters, only 15 percent had free girl characters. On average, adding a female character cost $7.53—even though the games themselves cost less than $1. In the Disney game *Temple Run Oz*, the only female character offered cost nearly $30! She wrote an article for *The Washington Post* newspaper and game companies took notice. *Temple Run* promised to add a free female character. Disney made its female character free as well. And the creators of the game *Noodles Now* even added a female character named Maddie!

CHAPTER 5

Make Your Game Come to Life

What do you notice about the look and sound of your favorite video game? Art, animation, music, sound, and special effects can make your games come to life! Of course, everything you see and hear in an electronic game has to be translated into code, from the characters' hairstyles to explosions.

Back when Atari introduced *Pong*, computer graphics were so primitive that the ball was just a small white square on a black screen. That's because when *Pong* was invented in 1972, electronics didn't have a lot of **computer memory**.

? **ESSENTIAL QUESTION**

Why are the looks and sounds of a game important? Can you make a game more fun just by changing the look and sound?

WORDS TO KNOW

computer memory: the part of an electronic device that stores information so that it can be reached quickly when needed.

When you look at a computer screen, what you're really seeing is a grid made up of thousands and thousands of **pixels**. These are small squares of color. On the old black-and-white or black-and-green screens, each pixel only had two choices of color.

To save memory and help games run faster, early video game images also had low **resolution**. That meant screens were divided into so few pixels that they were large enough to see.

pixel: short for "picture element," one of the small squares of color used to show an image on a digital screen.

resolution: the degree of sharpness and detail in an image, measured in pixels.

WORDS TO KNOW

The low resolution of the images made them look blocky.

When colors were introduced, games used only a few. The number code for each color, as with everything else, had to be saved in the computer's memory.

PS

TRY PLAYING *PONG* YOURSELF!

Pong was invented as a training exercise by an employee at Atari named Allan Alcorn. The owner of Atari, Nolan Bushnell, decided to see if the public liked it as much as his employees. He installed it at a local restaurant and it was incredibly popular! How is *Pong* different from the games you usually play? What is different about the graphics and the sound?

Play Pong 🔍

two-dimensional (2-D): something that appears flat and can only be measured in two directions, length (how long it is) and width (how wide it is).

three-dimensional (3-D): something that appears solid and can be measured in three directions, length, width, and depth (how deep it is, how far back it goes).

high definition (HD): a better level of clarity for digital screen images than had been the standard before.

8-bit: a style of pixilated art, based on the look of early video games.

retro: a style of graphics that looks like an early video game, with low resolution and blocky pixels.

voxel: short for "volume pixels," a 3-D style of pixel.

WORDS TO KNOW

Because of the limitations of computer memory, the first games were **two-dimensional (2-D)**. Objects could be seen from only one angle at a time. Platform jumpers and side-scrollers showed the action from the side. Shooters usually showed the action from above as a maze or map.

BONUS POINTS

As the resolution of computer screens improved, characters and objects could be more detailed and **three-dimensional (3-D)**. Most modern, **high-definition (HD)** console and computer games feature realistic artwork, lifelike animation, and special effects, just like those in high-budget action films.

Some games today still use the blocky **8-bit** style because it gives them a **retro** look. Have you spent time in a *Minecraft* world? *Minecraft* gets its unique style by using a 3-D version of pixels known as **voxels** that combine the old-fashioned look with up-to-date graphics.

HOW IS VIDEO GAME ART CREATED?

Before you even start drawing your characters, objects, and backgrounds, you have to figure out how they all fit together. Thinking like an architect will help you design your game's levels.

Instead of creating real-life buildings, you're building playspaces for players to run through.

Your design should also give players hints about which way to go. That's why your design document includes maps that show where characters and objects can move.

Video game art starts as sketches drawn on paper or directly on the computer or tablet using a touch screen. If your game is 3-D, players can see the backs, sides, tops, and bottoms of objects and backgrounds, so you need to draw those different views as well.

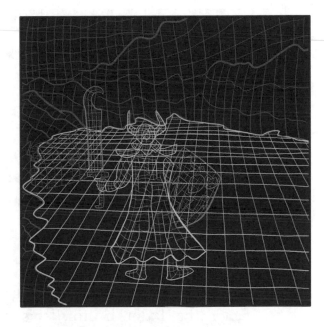

Then you can use special software to combine the different angles and create a blank 3-D shell of the character, object, or background, called a mesh. This mesh can be covered with skins of different textures as needed, like putting wrapping paper on a present. This is called texture mapping.

The same technique is used to make 2-D or 3-D drawings move. Have you ever used a flipbook? When you flip quickly through the pages, you can watch drawn characters move! Or at least they look like they're moving.

WHAT IS A GAME ENGINE?

A **game engine** is a ready-made computer program that serves as a framework to make all the parts of a video game work together. It lets designers focus on gameplay, characters, and other things that make their game different from the rest.

Some companies build their own, but a few of the most popular game engines, such as Unreal Engine and Unity, can be used for free. The owners ask only that you pay them a fee if your game makes money.

game engine: a computer program that serves as a framework to make all the parts of a video game work together.

WORDS TO KNOW

Animated images are series of slightly different drawings that flash on the screen very quickly. Your brain makes you see these separate drawings as one object moving smoothly through space. Once the software knows what your character looks like from different views, you can move it around like a digital puppet.

ART IN SCRATCH PAINT EDITOR

With Scratch, you can change the look of sprites and backdrops using the Paint Editor. This opens automatically when you select a Sprite and click on the Costumes Tab above the Blocks Palette. The Paint Editor even lets you create a new sprite by clicking on the paintbrush in the editing bar above the Sprite List.

You can upload your own drawings or photographs or draw right in the program. Although it's very basic, this is a good introduction to the more advanced graphic design software you might try someday.

The Paint Editor lets you work with two different kinds of images—vector and bitmap. Think of a **vector image** as a shape filled with a smooth layer of color. It will always have nice sharp lines, edges, and colors. In the computer's own language, a vector image is described in terms of the 2-D shape. Control points along the sides let you push or pull on the shape, like working on a slab of stretchy putty.

WORDS TO KNOW

vector image: a digital image that is saved in the computer's memory as points, lines, and shapes.

bitmap image: a digital image saved in the computer's memory as a grid of pixels.

To create a sprite or backdrop design using vector mode, you layer different shapes on top of each other. If you want to draw an eye, first make a white oval, and then a colored circle. Each shape stays in its own layer unless you group them together. That means you can make the eye look to the left or right just by dragging the colored circle back and forth on top of the white oval. You can also switch layers around to overlap one shape or object behind the other.

A **bitmap image**, on the other hand, is described pixel by pixel. A bitmap of an American flag would describe where each red, white, or blue pixel would go. Photographs are bitmap images. A bitmap image gives you a lot of control for adding details. But if you try to enlarge it, it will start to look blocky.

BONUS POINTS

For more tips on how to use the Paint Editor, check out the Scratch Help video tutorials.

Scratch help videos 🔍

When you open the Paint Editor, the vector toolbar is along the right edge of the workspace and the bitmap toolbar is along the left. The icons tell you what each tool does. You can draw using lines, rectangles, or ellipses. A paint bucket will fill any closed shape with the color you choose. It also lets you choose a fade effect that can make a flat image look 3-D. An eraser lets you delete parts you don't want and a rubber stamp lets you copy and duplicate.

You can switch back and forth from vector to bitmap by clicking the button on the bottom right. That's a good way to understand how the two modes differ.

BONUS POINTS

"Scratching" is a term DJs use to describe moving a record back and forth on a turntable to produce scratchy sounds. In Scratch you take different bits of code and put them together to make something new.

THE MUSIC OF VIDEO GAMES

Music in a video game can add to the experience of playing games in many ways. Here are some tips for choosing or writing great game music.

Use music to set the scene. If it's a sunny meadow, try light, happy music that bounces along. For a scene set in a dungeon, lay on a few slow, heavy chords to build tension. Music can also help set the pace. A quick, steady beat can make a race scene more thrilling or it can push the player to move faster through a dangerous maze.

Pick one style of music throughout. Use music to pull together the different levels of your game. If there are characters who enter, exit, and reappear on different levels, give them each their own tune to signal their presence.

Loop short pieces of music. Music takes a lot of computer memory, so most games use short melodies that loop over and over. For your repeating melodies, try to keep the ending similar to the beginning, so it won't distract your players when it starts over. Make repeating melodies interesting by adding multiple layers. Start with the pounding of the beat, then the next time around add a melody line to help increase excitement.

Keep your music simple. If you decide to add a theme song to the beginning or end of your game, keep it short, simple, and to the point. What's your favorite part of your game? That's what the song should be about!

PLANNING YOUR USER INTERFACE

Another part of designing the look of a video game includes the UI, the user interface. A video game screen has to show the controls, the score, the experience bar, and other signs of how the players are doing and what they are supposed to do next. One planning tool for this is a **wireframe**. This is a diagram of the screen that shows where various information boxes will be located. A wireframe in your design document will help you and your team members create a UI that players can quickly figure out.

WORDS TO KNOW

wireframe: a blueprint that shows the arrangement of content on the screen.

ADD SOUND AND MUSIC IN SCRATCH

As you've already seen, you can add sound effects and music to your script from the Scratch library with the light purple Sound blocks. Scratch also lets you record music or sound to use for your projects or upload music files from your computer. If you use a recording that you did not write and play yourself, check that the creator has given the public permission to use it. You might have to find his or her contact information and request permission.

**You can edit your sound files
using the Sound Editor.**

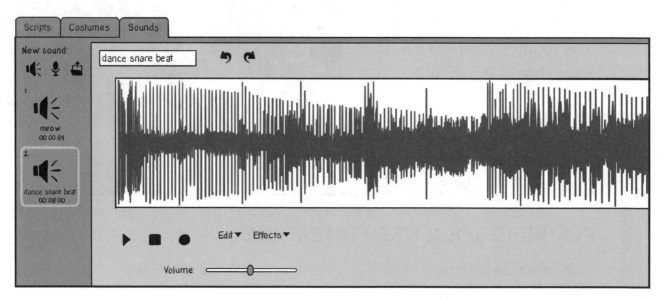

Select a sound and click on the Sounds Tab above the Blocks Palette to open an editing area with a long black shape. This represents the sound being played. It gets wider and narrower depending on the volume. You can highlight portions of the shape to copy or delete, and you can even reverse them.

You can also create your own music, note by note. The "set instrument" block has a pull-down menu of more than 20 different instruments. The choices include electronic music in 8-bit style, also known as **chiptune**.

To hear what these sound like, drag the block to the Scripts Area and add a "play note" block underneath. To pick the note you want, you need to choose or type in its **MIDI (Musical Instrument Digital Interface)** code number. A small piano keyboard pops up to make it easier. To play a song, just keep stacking "play note" blocks. Other blocks let you control the volume and the **tempo**. There is also a "play drum" block with its own menu of drums and related instruments.

chiptune: a type of electronic music based on the music used in early video games.

MIDI (Musical Instrument Digital Interface): computer code that tells a device what notes to play.

tempo: the pace at which a musical piece is played.

hardware: the physical parts of an electronic device such as the case, keyboard, screen, and speakers.

WORDS TO KNOW

BONUS POINTS

Video game music isn't just for your headphones anymore. Orchestras around the world are adapting the most famous theme songs for concerts—such as *The Legend of Zelda: Symphony of the Goddesses*—and selling more tickets than the opera!

Legend of Zelda opera 🔍

RAMP UP YOUR GAME WITH HARDWARE

Using **hardware** is another way to make games even more fun. Even before the Wii let players use controllers that look like tennis rackets and golf clubs, peripherals such as steering wheels for racing games made players feel as though they were more a part of the action.

haptics: the use of vibrations in a smartphone or game controller to make it seem as though you can feel the movement happening on the screen.

WORDS TO KNOW

The use of haptic technology that makes your smartphone or game controller vibrate can fool your brain into thinking you're moving a real object around.

Augmented reality devices, such as the Microsoft HoloLens, blend 3-D characters and objects with a view of the room you're in. Virtual reality devices you wear over your eyes, such as the standalone Oculus Rift or Sony's Project Morpheus for the PS4, due to come out in 2016, create the illusion that you are surrounded by the game itself. They make BASE jumping games such as *AaaaaAAaaaAAAaaAAAAaAAAAA!!! A Reckless Disregard for Gravity* even more thrilling!

You can even create your own game controllers. A fun device called MaKey MaKey plugs into your computer and has wires that you attach to things that work like the keys on your keyboard. Kids have built MaKey MaKey controllers out of bananas, aluminum foil, or even bowls of water.

BONUS POINTS

Visit the MaKey MaKey website to get ideas for hardware.

MaKey MaKey 🔍

Try using different hardware to play a Scratch version of *Simon*.

Scratch Simon game 🔍

MaKey MaKey controllers work well for games you build in. For instance, you could use a MaKey MaKey with a Scratch version of the game *Simon*. Instead of pressing the buttons that light up on the *Simon* device, you could make your own buttons out of paper, fabric, or even lumps of modeling dough!

YOUR OWN OCULUS

You can also make your own Oculus Rift–style virtual reality headset with just a smartphone and a little cardboard. Google Cardboard is a holder you can buy as a kit or just cut out using free pattern pieces. Fold it up, insert your smartphone and hold it up to your eyes. It becomes a quick, easy, and cheap way to play virtual reality games!

Google Cardboard 🔍

PLAY WITH TIME, SPACE, AND GRAVITY

One of the fun things about making video games is creating your own world within the computer. You can even invent your own laws of science! Make time speed up or slow down, stretch space or squash it, or make the pull of gravity stronger or weaker than it is on Earth.

When you fling an *Angry Bird* across the screen with a slingshot, it curves up and falls back to the ground, knocking over building blocks and green pigs. But the path the bird takes through the air is not quite the same as it would be in real life.

In the game *Portal*, if you jump into a blue hole in the floor, you may pop out of an orange hole in the wall. It's as if gravity were pulling you sideways instead of down.

Other actions in *Portal* defy the laws of gravity as well. But while objects behave differently in a video game world, they still have to follow their own rules.

Part of the challenge for the player is figuring out what those rules are, so when you fling a bird or jump through a portal, you have a pretty good idea of where you will end up.

The piece of code controlling all those rules is called a **physics engine**. Many games use a premade physics engine, which can save valuable programming time and energy. The "bounce" command in Scratch is an example of a premade physics engine.

You've learned how to come up with a video game concept, write the code to make it run, and add the design details that make it unique and interesting. But what does it take to get a game out into the world, where anybody can play it? Find out in the next chapter!

WORDS TO KNOW

physics engine: the software that controls how objects in the game react to gravity and other forces.

? ESSENTIAL QUESTION

Now it's time to consider and discuss the Essential Question: Why are the looks and sounds of a game important? Can you make a game more fun just by changing the look and sound?

PHYSICS ENGINE IN SCRATCH

Now that you know how to make a bouncing ball in Scratch, tinker with the laws of physics to see how the action changes.

1 Open the Scratch Cat Dodge Ball game you created in Chapter 4. You can also start a new project using the bouncing ball script from that game or remix one created by the author. You'll find the author's game by going to scratch.mit.edu/projects/47856170.

2 Experiment with different ways to change the physics of your game. For instance, what happens if you do these things differently?

- increase or decrease the number of steps the ball moves
- make the ball bigger or smaller
- add additional balls
- add a command to make the balls fly off in different directions if they bump into each other

3 You can make your own physics engine by copying your script and using it in other games. To copy code to use in a different sprite or a different game, drag it to the Backpack on the bottom of the Scratch screen. The Backpack is only visible when you are signed into your Scratch account online.

MEMORY GAME IN SCRATCH

In this activity you'll build a *Sprite Clones Memory Game* in Scratch. It's a memory game remixed from a game by Al Sweigart. You start with a screen full of identical sprites placed randomly around the stage. To clear the level, you must click on each sprite one by one in the correct order. When you click on the right sprite, it lights up. If it's the wrong sprite, it signals you by jiggling and then all the changed sprites go back to their original appearance. Once the game is built, you'll reskin it to make it your own.

To save time and get right to reskinning the game, start with the version on Scratch created by the author. Go to scratch.mit.edu/projects/33789122 or type "Sprite Clones Memory Game" into the Scratch search box. If you choose this path, begin with step 9 on page 106.

To code the entire game, you'll start by coding three scripts for the backdrop.

- The first script **broadcasts** a message called *reset* to all the other scripts to tell the game to start a new level. It also creates a variable called *Count* that tells the game how many sprites to show for each level, starting with three sprites.

- The second script tells the program to create a variable called *Next* that tells the game which sprite comes next in the pattern for that level of the game.

- The third script tells the game to go to the next level when it receives a win message.

BONUS POINTS

Al Sweigart is a software developer who has written several books for young people on making video games in Python. He makes programming fun and accessible for all ages. You can check him out on the Scratch website.

Al Sweigart Scratch 🔍

WORDS TO KNOW

broadcast: in Scratch, sending a message to blocks in every script for every sprite.

1 Follow these steps to code the first backdrop script.

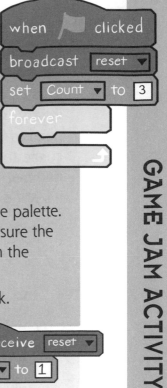

- From Events, drag *when [flag] clicked* to the Scripts Area.

- Go down the palette to *broadcast [ ]*. Click on the drop down arrow, and select *new message*. In the pop-up box, type in *reset*. Drag it to the bottom of the first block.

- From Data, click *Make a Variable*. Call the variable *Count*. Uncheck the box in front of it in the palette so that it doesn't show up on the stage. Four new blocks appear in the palette. Drag the *set [ ] to [ ]* block to the bottom of the stack. Make sure the variable in the window is *Count*. Then click on the number in the block and type 3.

- From Control, drag a *forever* block to the bottom of the stack.

2 To code the second backdrop script.

- From Events, drag *when I receive [reset]* over to the Scripts Area.

- From Data, drag a *set [ ] to [ ]* block to the bottom of the stack. Choose *Next* as the variable, and type *1* in the white window.

3 To code the third backdrop script.

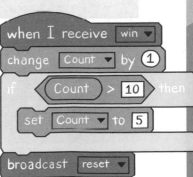

- From Events, get a *when I receive [ ]* block and create a message called *win*.

- From Data, go to the *change* block, set the window to *Count*, and snap it to the last block.

- From Control, drag over an *if [ ] then* block.

- From Operators, drag a *greater than (>)* block to the Scripts Area and plug it into the diamond window on the *if [ ] then* block.

- From Data, drag an oval *Count* block into the first white window in the > block. In the second white window, type *10*.

- From Data, drag a *set [ ] to [ ]* block inside the mouth of the *if [ ] then* block. Choose the *Count* variable, and in the white window type in *5*.

- From Events, drag *broadcast [reset]* to the bottom of the stack.

PROJECT CONTINUES ON NEXT PAGE

4 The sprite to use for this game is the little yellow alien Gobo. Delete the Sprite Cat and add Gobo from the sprite library. Your game will have 10 sprites, but you only need to write scripts for the first one. Then just clone it to create the others. The first script gives each sprite its own number, places it in a random spot on the stage, and makes sure it's not overlapping another sprite.

- From Events, drag *when [flag] clicked* to the Scripts Area.

- From Data, create a variable called *Number*. In the popup box, click *For this sprite only*. Be sure to uncheck the box on the palette. Drag the *set [ ] to [ ]* block under the first block. Choose the variable Number and type *1* in the white window.

- From Motion, drag a *go to x: [ ] y:[ ]* block to the bottom of the stack. From Operators (light green), insert a *pick random [ ] to [ ]* block into the white window after *x:* in the *go to* block. Type in the numbers -200 and 200. Do the same with the *y:* window, and set those numbers to *-140* and *140*.

- From Control, drag an *if [ ] then* block to the Scripts Area.

- From Sensing, insert a *touching color [ ]?* block into the window of the *if [ ] then* block. Then click on the color box. As you move your mouse around, you will see the color in the box change. Click on Gobo to turn the box yellow.

- From Motion, drag a *change x by [ ]* and a *change y by [ ]* block into the opening of the *if [ ] then* block. Type *10* in the white windows.

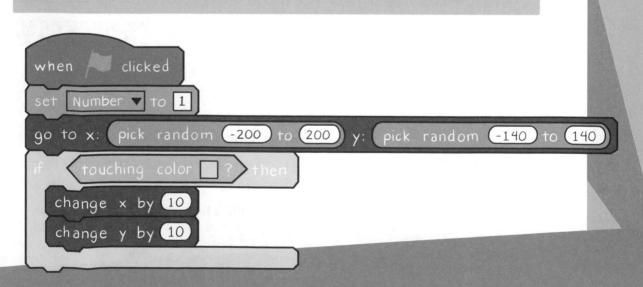

5 The second script moves the sprite to a new location for each level. You can copy some of the code from the first script to save time.

- From Events, drag a *when I receive [ ]* block to the Scripts Area and set the message to *win*.

- Go to the first script, click on the *go to* block, and pull it down. All the blocks below it should come away too. Right-click on just these blocks and choose *duplicate*. Then put the first script back together, and move the duplicate blocks under the *when I receive [ ]* block.

→ Copied from previous script

```
when I receive win ▼
go to x: pick random -200 to 200 y: pick random -140 to 140
if    touching color ☐ ?    then
    change x by 10
    change y by 10
```

```
when I receive reset ▼
set brightness ▼ effect to -75
if    Count > Number    then
    show
else
    hide
```

6 The third script makes the sprite dark at the start of each new level and hides sprites that are not needed for that level.

- From Events, drag over a *when I receive [ ]* block set to *reset*.

- From Looks, drag a *set [ ] effect to [ ]* block under the first block. Choose *brightness* and type in *-75* in the white window.

- From Control, drag an *if [ ] then else* block to the bottom of the stack.

- From Operators, insert a *greater than* block into the *if [ ] then else* block.

- From Data, insert *Count* into the first white window and *Number* into the second on the greater than block.

- From Looks, drag *show* into the mouth-like opening under *if* and *hide* into the opening under *else*.

PROJECT CONTINUES ON NEXT PAGE

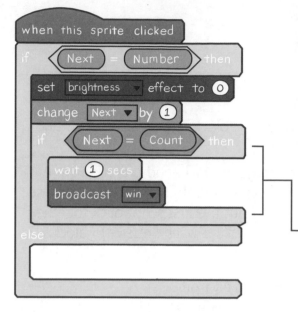

nest: in computer programming, putting one conditional statement inside another. Loops can also be nested.

Example of a nested statement—an *if [ ] then* block within an *if [ ] then* block.

7 The fourth script makes the sprite light up if it is clicked and tells the game to go on to find the next sprite if it is the correct one. If not, the sprite jiggles and the level is reset. This script contains **nested** statements—one conditional statement inside another.

- From Events, start with *when this sprite is clicked*.
- From Control, add an *if [ ] then else* block.
- From Operators, insert an *equals* block in the window after *if*. From Data, insert *Next* in the first window and *Number* in the second.
- From Looks, drag *set [ ] effect to [ ]* into the *if* opening (the top opening in the *if [ ] then else* block) and set it to *brightness* and *0*.
- From Data, drag *change [ ] by [ ]* under the brightness block. Set the variable to *Next* and the number to *1*. *Change* means the number listed is added to the variable.
- From Control, drag an *if [ ] then* block under the *change by* block.
- From Operators, insert an *equals* block into the *if [ ] then* block window.
- From Data, insert *Next* into the first window in the *equals* block and *Count* into the other.
- From Control, drag *wait [ ] secs* to the *if then* opening. Set it to *1*.
- From Events, drag a *broadcast* block under *wait*. Set it to *win*.

ALMOST DONE! THIS STEP CONTINUES . . .

- From Control, drag a *repeat [ ]* block into the *else* opening. Set it to *2*.

- From Motion, drag a *glide [ ] secs to x: [ ] y: [ ]* block into the opening of the *repeat* block. Set the first window to *0.05*. Drag an *x position* block into the second window, after *x:*.

- From Operators, drag a *plus* block (*[ ] = [ ]*) into the third window, after the *y:* in the glide block.

- From Motion, drag *y position* into the first window in the *plus* block. Type in *10* in the second window.

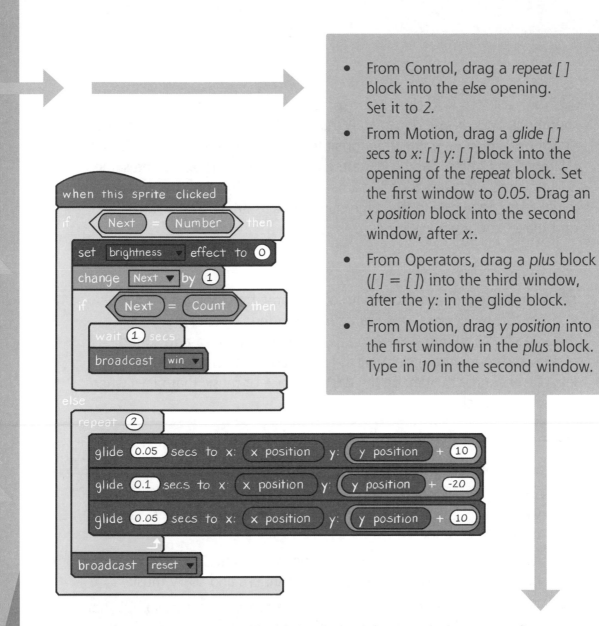

- Make two copies of the *glide* block you just built by right-clicking directly on it and choosing *duplicate*. Stack them under the first. In the middle copy, type in *0.1* in the secs window, and *-20* in the y position window. Leave the bottom copy as is.

- From Events, drag a *broadcast [reset]* block under the repeat block but still inside the *else* window of the *if [ ] then else* block.

PROJECT CONTINUES ON NEXT PAGE

8 Your last step is to clone your sprite. Right click on the Sprite1 thumbnail and choose *duplicate*. A thumbnail labeled Sprite2 will appear. You must click on the new thumbnail to see its script! Now go to the *set [Number] to [ ]* block, and change the number shown to *2*. Do the same 8 more times, for a total of 10 sprites, making sure to set the Number variable for each one to the same number as its name. Test your game and make sure it works!

9 Now it's time to add some life to the game by changing the sprites and backdrops. Choose new characters from the Scratch library or use the Scratch Paint Editor to create your own. You can also add sound effects and music using the Scratch Sound Editor, such as a sound that lets players know they made the wrong choice or music that plays when they clear a level.

Here are some ideas to get you started.

- Create an underwater game using starfish sprites, a backdrop of the ocean floor, and music that sounds like water dripping.

- Give it a space theme with UFO sprites, laser sound effects, and a backdrop of stars.

- Make a spooky version featuring zombies or bats, set against a backdrop of a cave or graveyard with shrieks and scary music.

- Design a version set in a barnyard with goats or pigs as sprites that make animal noises when you click on them.

10 As you make changes, be sure to look for bugs that might appear in your code. For instance, the piece of script that makes the sprites shift a little if they are overlapping only works if they are touching something that is yellow.

DRAW YOUR OWN 8-BIT GRAPH PAPER ART

IDEAS FOR SUPPLIES

graph paper ❖ *colored pencils*

You can use a bitmap drawing program to create 8-bit art, but you can also draw it by hand. The secret is graph paper, which is paper printed with grids. Treat each box on the grid as a pixel and it's easy to make pixelated art! How simple can you make your drawing and still be able to tell what it is?

1 There are different ways to create your own 8-bit art. One method is to make a copy of a picture you'd like to convert to 8-bit. Slide it under the piece of graph paper and use a little tape to hold them both in place. Draw around the outside of your image following along the lines on the graph paper! Do the same for any details you want to include. Then color in the areas you have outlined.

2 You can also "doodle" with 8-bit art. Draw something from your imagination, again following the graph paper lines. Or just put your pencil on one printed line and start building random shapes. After a few minutes, your doodle might start to look like a mushroom or castle or sword. Keep adding details and see what kind of picture emerges!

TRY THIS: Make 8-bit art from a photograph. Slide a color photo underneath your graph paper and trace the images by following the lines of the graph paper. Color it in. How does it look different? Are the images still recognizable?

CHAPTER 6

So, You Want to Make Video Games

Creating a great game is only one part of being a game designer. Once you've tested it on your friends and family, it's time to share your game with a wider audience. Who knows, your game might become the next *Flappy Bird*—a viral hit that every gamer wants to play! Find out how you can release a game to the public and what it takes to become a game design professional.

MAKING YOUR OWN GAMES NOW

The best way to get into games is to go ahead and start making them. Some game designers get their start by building mods or new levels for existing games that catch the attention of a game studio. But today, it's also easy for indie designers to build and release games themselves.

? **ESSENTIAL QUESTION**

What can you do now to become a game designer?

Here are some kid-friendly places to start.

Scratch: The online Scratch community is a great learning resource and a place to get feedback and find ideas to make your games better. Create an account and you can easily publish your game by hitting the Share button at the top of the screen.

Gamestar Mechanic: Although you need to pay a fee to access everything this instructional site for kids has to offer, the first game design challenge and its showcase are free.

Construct2: The free version of this game-building platform has its own Arcade, where you can share your game. It also lets you upload games to Amazon.com.

GameSalad: Another drag-and-drop environment with a free version that lets you build games for iOS and Android devices as well as computers.

A great way to get attention for your games is to take part in a game jam. Libraries and colleges sometimes host their own game jams.

There's also the Global Game Jam (GGJ), a yearly event that takes place during one weekend at locations around the world. Participants work together during 48 hours to design, develop, create, and test a new game based on a theme. The GGJ is not a competition. Anyone can join in, no matter what their level of game design experience.

In January 2014, GGJ participants at 488 locations in 72 countries built more than 4,000 games!

GET SCHOOLED IN GAME DESIGN

It takes a lot of different skills and knowledge about a wide range of areas to make a video game. Many game design professionals get their start by studying game-related subjects in school. You can even major in game design and development in college!

Want to improve your chances for getting into a good game design college program? "Love math. You can never have enough math!" says David Schwartz, the undergraduate program coordinator for the School of Interactive Games & Media at the Rochester Institute of Technology (RIT).

It's also helpful to take computer programming and computer graphics classes to understand what those tools can do. And it helps to have a broad background. "Most game designers know a lot of stuff," says Schwartz.

BONUS POINTS

David Schwartz says the most important thing to keep in mind with game design is to always be curious, "Go beyond the minimum. Constantly question, constantly go beyond."

VIDEO GAME CHALLENGE

The National STEM Video Game Challenge was launched in September 2010 at the White House by President Barack Obama. Through the years, thousands of entries have been submitted by U.S. middle and high school students. Contestants submit game design documents or game prototypes they created using game creation platforms such as Scratch, Gamestar Mechanic, Unity, and GameMaker. Prizes include computer hardware, game design and educational software, and cash awards.

National STEM challenge 🔍

GET READY FOR THE WORLD OF GAME DESIGN!

Andy Phelps is founder of the School of Interactive Games & Media at RIT and director of the college's MAGIC Center, which helps students make and market games. Phelps says there's no better time in the history of games for people to get involved. "For the first time, games are part of the mass culture," he says, "and they will continue to be a vibrant part for a long time to come."

His advice for kids who want to learn more about the world of video games? "Keep a little journal next to you. Reflect on your play. Write it down so you can compare it the next time you play it." Here are some of the questions you should ask yourself.

- What are your expectations?
- Why did you pick this game?
- Why are you excited to play it?
- Who are you in the game?
- What is your goal?
- What's the experience like?
- How does the game help you to understand how it works?
- What do you like or not like?
- If you could change it, what would you change?

He also suggests reading about game developers in books, magazines, and websites. But most importantly:

"Start making games!"

? ESSENTIAL QUESTION

Now it's time to consider and discuss the Essential Question: What can you do now to become a game designer?

HOLD YOUR OWN GAME JAM

IDEAS FOR SUPPLIES

device with game-building software (one per person or team) ❖ adults who can help with software questions and game design

Do you have a group of friends who have always wanted to make a game together? Or perhaps your school or library would like to hold an event for gamers. You might even be looking for a unique idea for a party. Holding your own game jam may be just the thing you need!

1 Write up a schedule so you have enough time to plan, build, test, and share your games. A game jam can last a couple of hours or a couple of days. Set a timer so you stick to your schedule.

2 Come up with an idea for your game. Discuss the theme of the game jam with your team members or other game designers. You may need to look up information to help you make your game more interesting.

3 Make as simple a prototype as you can and start testing your game. When you've got it working, add twists to make it more interesting to play.

4 Be sure to leave time at the end to share your games with other game jam participants. Everyone may not end up with a finished game, and that's okay. You may want to give prizes for games in categories such as "most inventive," "best battle," and "best story." You can also make up certificates for everyone who took part. Have fun!

8-bit: a style of pixilated art, based on the look of early video games.

achievable challenge: a goal that is within reach, but only with effort.

addictive: causing a strong and harmful need to do something.

algorithm: a series of steps to complete a task. There can be different algorithms to do the same thing.

arcade: an amusement area with games you play by inserting money or tokens. Arcade games sometimes award tickets you can exchange for toys and other prizes.

augmented reality game: a game that inserts real-world images into the game environment or interacts with real-world objects.

backdrop: a design that can be applied to the stage on the Scratch UI.

BCE: put after a date, BCE stands for Before Common Era and counts down to zero. CE stands for Common Era and counts up from zero. The year this book is published is 2015 CE.

binary: a math system containing only zeroes and ones. The word binary comes from the Latin word *bi* for "two," as in bicycle and binoculars.

bit: the basic unit of information storage in a computer, consisting of a zero or a one.

bitmap image: a digital image saved in the computer's memory as a grid of pixels.

block: a puzzle-piece shape that is used to create code in Scratch.

Boolean logic: named after George Boole, to turn every decision a computer makes into a yes or no question.

bosses: the main enemy in one level of a game that must be defeated to move on.

brainstorm: to come up with a bunch of ideas quickly and without judgment.

broadcast: in Scratch, sending a message to blocks in every script for every sprite.

bug: a mistake in the code that causes unexpected problems.

byte: a group of eight bits that is treated as a single piece of information.

call a function: to tell the computer program to run a function.

cheat codes: keyboard commands that let you skip steps or give you extra powers.

chemistry: the science of how substances interact, combine, and change.

chiptune: a type of electronic music based on the music used in early video games.

command: an instruction in the form of code that tells a computer to do something. Also called a statement.

computer memory: the part of an electronic device that stores information so that it can be reached quickly when needed.

conditional scripting: the part of a script or plan for a game that shows what happens when a player makes one choice or another.

conditional statement: a step in a program that gives a computer two choices depending on whether the answer to a certain test is yes or no.

console: a specialized computer used to play video games on a TV screen.

controller: a part or device that players use to interact with a game.

cosplay: dressing up in the costume of a character from a video game, movie, etc., for a special event.

costume: a variation of a sprite that looks somewhat different than the original.

data: information, usually given in the form of numbers, that can be processed by a computer.

define a function: to tell the computer what steps a function contains.

degree: a measurement used for angles and circles. A circle is divided into 360 degrees.

design document: a guide for the team that will be working on the game, containing all the details and plans.

documentation: an explanation of a section of computer code, written in non-machine language.

dopamine: a chemical in the brain that improves your mood and lowers stress.

drag-and-drop: clicking on an object and holding a button on your mouse while you move it to the desired spot.

Easter egg: a secret message or surprise hidden in a video game for players to find.

endorphin: a neurotransmitter that masks pain.

experience points (XP): points you accumulate toward your goal, often shown as a long narrow bar.

fan art: artwork made by a fan of a game, movie, comic book, etc.

feedback: information about how you are doing.

flowchart: a diagram that shows all the possible options and results.

function: a short piece of code that is given a name so it can be used multiple times in a program simply by inserting the name. Also called a subroutine or procedure.

game assets: any part of the game that the player can see or interact with directly, including characters, objects, backgrounds, text, sound, and special effects.

game engine: a computer program that serves as a framework to make all the parts of a video game work together.

Game jam: a gathering of game developers to design and create games in a short period of time.

gameplay: the way players interact with a game and the experience it provides. Game reviewers use it to rate how well they liked playing the game.

gamer: someone who loves to play games.

gamification: adding game elements to another kind of activity to make it more fun or appealing.

geometry: a branch of mathematics that deals with points, lines, and shapes and where they are in space.

graphics: the images on a computer screen, including a game's characters and background.

hack: finding a new and different way to use or control something.

haptics: the use of vibrations in a smartphone or game controller to make it seem as though you can feel the movement happening on the screen.

hardware: the physical parts of an electronic device such as the case, keyboard, screen, and speakers.

high definition (HD): a better level of clarity for digital screen images than had been the standard before.

horizontal: going straight across from side to side.

hormone: a chemical that carries signals from one part of the body to another.

IF-THEN-ELSE statement: a command that tells the computer to test whether a certain condition is true, then either go on to the next step or else a different step depending on the result of the test.

in-app purchase: an item that you buy with real money to use in video games.

innovation: a new invention or way of doing something.

iteration: using a process that repeats itself, in this case, developing a game, testing it, developing it further, and testing it again.

joystick: a control lever that can be pushed in different directions.

level up: to achieve the next level by earning a certain amount of XP.

logic gate: a test that results in only one true-or-false answer.

loop: a section of code that is repeated a certain number of times or until a specific condition is met.

machine language: the code used directly by a computer, written in zeroes and ones.

massively multiplayer online (MMO): an online role-playing game in which large numbers of players all take part in the same game.

mass produce: to manufacture large amounts of a product.

microtransaction: a very small online payment.

MIDI (Musical Instrument Digital Interface): computer code that tells a device what notes to play.

minifig: a Lego minifigure.

mission: one of the goals players must complete to advance in the game.

mobile game: a game that can be played on a mobile device such as a smartphone or tablet.

mod: to modify a game to create new levels, characters, or objects or make a new version, when done by a fan rather than a company.

narrative: something that has the form of a story.

nest: in computer programming, putting one conditional statement inside another. Loops can also be nested.

neurotransmitter: a chemical that carries signals between parts of the brain.

non-playable characters (NPC): characters in a video game that are controlled by the computer program, not including enemies.

object of the game: what you have to do to win or reach the final goal, also called the objective.

oscilloscope: a device that measures electrical signals and shows them as wavy lines.

oxytocin: a hormone that makes you happy when you interact with people you like.

physics engine: the software that controls how objects in the game react to gravity and other forces.

pixel: short for "picture element," one of the small squares of color used to show an image on a digital screen.

playable characters (PC): characters or avatars in a video game that are controlled by the players.

playtest: a research session where players are asked to play an unfinished game while the designers take notes on how it works and players' comments and reactions.

plot: the events that happen in a story.

power-up: an object that gives a character more ability or strength.

programmer: a person who writes computer programs. Also called a coder.

programming language: a language invented to communicate instructions to a computer.

prototype: an early version of a design used for testing.

pseudocode: from the Greek word for false, this is an algorithm written in language a human can read and understand.

psychology: the study of how people think, behave, and feel.

quality assurance (QA): playing a game that is nearly finished to find any problems before it is published.

quest: a search or challenge a player must complete to level-up or win a game.

reskin: adding new graphics and other design elements to the structure underneath an existing game.

resolution: the degree of sharpness and detail in an image, measured in pixels.

retro: a style of graphics that looks like an early video game, with low resolution and blocky pixels.

role-playing game (RPG): a game, usually with a fantasy setting, where players' actions reflect the characters they play in the story.

script: the name for a computer program that a user can write in Scratch.

sequence of commands: the order of the steps in a program.

serotonin: a neurotransmitter that makes you alert and responds to light levels.

software: another name for a computer program that tells the computer what to do.

sprite: an object or character.

stage: the background of a Scratch project.

string: a short group of letters or words that is used as data.

Supreme Court of the United States: the highest court in the country, which reviews laws and decisions of lower courts.

syntax: the rules for writing commands in a programming language.

tempo: the pace at which a musical piece is played.

text adventure game: a game in which players go on a quest with only written directions to guide them.

three-dimensional (3-D): something that appears solid and can be measured in three directions, length, width, and depth (how deep it is, how far back it goes).

thumbnail: a small copy of an image on a computer, usually linked to the full-sized version.

toys-to-life: a type of game that includes playable action figures.

transistor: a small device that acts as an on/off switch to control the flow of electricity in a computer.

treatment: a short description of how the game works.

two-dimensional (2-D): something that appears flat and can only be measured in two directions, length (how long it is) and width (how wide it is).

user interface (UI): in Scratch, the screen where you build your project.

variable: a symbol that holds the place for information that may change each time a command runs.

vector image: a digital image that is saved in the computer's memory as points, lines, and shapes.

vertical: going straight up and down.

video game: a game that is played by controlling images on a screen. Also known as an electronic game or digital game.

virtual: a computer version of something real.

virtual reality game: a game designed for a wearable screen that makes players feel as though they are inside the game itself.

visual programming language (VPL): sometimes called graphical software, this is computer code that uses images such as blocks to create a program instead of typed-out commands.

voxel: short for "volume pixels," a 3-D style of pixel.

WHILE statement: a command that tells the computer to keep repeating a loop as long as a certain condition is true.

wiki: a free website that allows users to write and edit articles explaining a topic or range of topics.

wireframe: a blueprint that shows the arrangement of content on the screen.

world-building: designing an imaginary setting for your game to take place in, including the people or creatures that live there, how they move and communicate, and what the buildings and landscape look like.

x-axis: the horizontal line on a graph that passes through the center point (0,0). Points are measured by how far to the left or right of the y-axis they are.

xy coordinates: a pair of numbers written like this (x,y) that tell where a point is on a graph, measured from the x-axis and y-axis.

y-axis: the vertical line on a graph that passes through the center point (0,0). Points are measured by how far above or below the x-axis they are.

METRIC EQUIVALENTS

Use this chart to find the metric equivalents to the English measurements in this book. If you need to know a half measurement, divide by two. If you need to know twice the measurement, multiply by two. How do you find a quarter measurement? How do you find three times the measurement?

English	Metric
1 inch	2.5 centimeters
1 foot	30.5 centimeters
1 yard	0.9 meter
1 mile	1.6 kilometers
1 pound	0.5 kilogram
1 teaspoon	5 milliliters
1 tablespoon	15 milliliters
1 cup	237 milliliters

BOOKS

Help Your Kids With Computer Coding (DK Publishing, 2014)

Game Design Workshop: Designing, Prototyping And Playtesting Games by Tracy Fullerton, Christopher Swain, and Steven Hoffman (CRC Press, 2004)

Guinness World Records 2015: Gamer's Edition (Guinness World Records Limited, 2014)

Video Game Developer by Chris Jozefowicz (Gareth Stevens Publishing, 2009)

1001 Video Games You Must Play Before You Die by Tony Mott (Cassell Illustrated, 2013)

Game On: Have You Got What It Takes To Be A Video Game Developer? by Lisa Thompson (Compass Point Books, 2009)

Learn to Program with Scratch: A Visual Introduction to Programming with Games, Art, Science, and Math by Majed Marji (No Starch Press, 2014)

Reality is Broken: Why Games Make Us Better and How They Can Change the World by Jane McGonigal (The Penguin Press, 2011)

TEXT-BASED PROGRAMMING LANGUAGES

Java (oracle.com/technetwork/topics/newtojava): The New to Java site for installing and using this free, very popular programming language.

Python (python.org/about/gettingstarted): The Getting Started guide for using Python, which comes pre-installed on many newer computers.

VISUAL PROGRAMMING LANGUAGES

Scratch (scratch.mit.edu): A programming language and online community from MIT where beginners can create interactive stories, games, and animations and share them with others around the world.

Alice (alice.org): A free tool from Carnegie Mellon University that teaches fundamental programming concepts while creating animated movies and simple video games using 3-D objects and characters in a virtual world.

Kodu (kodugamelab.com): Kodu lets kids create games on the PC and Xbox via a simple visual programming language.

Hopscotch (gethopscotch.com): A drag-and-drop language for the iPad. The basic version is free, with in-app purchases for advanced lessons.

Tynker (tynker.com): Use drag-and-drop programing blocks to build custom web and mobile games, including side-scrollers, two-player, and physics games. Free projects and a six-hour course are available on the Hour of Code page.

GAME DEVELOPMENT ENVIRONMENTS FOR ALL LEVELS

GameMaker: Studio (yoyogames.com): Game development platform for beginners and professionals.

Unity (unity3d.com): Free development platform for creating 2-D and 3-D games, used by many professional game studios.

Construct (scirra.com): Professional-quality game development platform for 2-D games.

Unreal Engine (unrealengine.com): Free game development tools for 2-D mobile games and consoles, popular with professionals.

FREE SOFTWARE PROGRAMS FOR CREATING GAME ART

Make 8 Bit Art (make8bitart.com): A free, open-source, online pixel art tool that lets you draw designs and download them to your computer.

TuxPaint (tuxpaint.org): A simple, open source drawing program for children ages 3 to 12 that runs on your computer. Free downloads are available for Windows, Mac, and Linux. You might want to turn off the annoying sound effects.

Inkscape (inkscape.org): A free, open-source, professional-quality vector graphics editor for advanced users.

Microsoft Paint (windows.microsoft.com/en-us/windows7/products/features/paint): A basic graphics editor that comes free with Windows operating systems for computers and tablets.

Blender (blender.org): Open-source 3-D graphics program for advanced users. Free downloads are available for Windows, Mac, and Linux.

PROGRAMMING INSTRUCTION FOR KIDS

BBC Bitesize Computing Curriculum (bbc.co.uk/schools/0/computing): A range of online computer programming information and instructional games for elementary through high school age students.

Blockly Games (blockly-games.appspot.com): Free online educational games from Google that teach programming concepts, which prepare children for conventional text-based languages.

Code Combat (codecombat.com): Free online battle game that teaches Python, Javascript, and other text-based languages. Advanced levels available by paid subscription.

Code.org (code.org): Sponsor of the Hour of Code (hourofcode.com) and other free online courses for all ages, using several types of instructional software.

Codecademy (codecademy.com): Free online interactive coding tutorials in several text-based languages and through an app for mobile devices.

Gamestar Mechanic (gamestarmechanic.com): A game and community designed to teach kids 7 to 14 the principles of game design and systems thinking in a highly engaging environment.

Invent with Scratch (inventwithscratch.com): Video tutorials by software developer Albert Sweigart, creator of the *Sprite Clones Memory Game*. Also find links to his free online ebooks, including *Invent Your Own Computer Games with Python* (inventwithpython.com).

Khan Academy (khanacademy.org/computing/cs): Free computer science video lessons in text-based languages, including advanced lessons in game-building.

Lightbot (lightbot.com): A drag-and-drop maze game that teaches programming and functions. Basic lessons are free online; a low-cost app is also available.

LittleBigPlanet 2 (littlebigplanet.playstation.com/en/games/littlebigplanet-2): Within this PlayStation game you can create levels, redefine the playing field, and make whole games.

GAMEMAKING EVENTS AND COMPETITIONS

Global Game Jam (globalgamejam.org): A yearly weekend-long event held at locations around the world.

National STEM Video Game Challenge (stemchallenge.org): A contest for U.S. middle and high school students.

Ludum Dare (ludumdare.com): The longest-running, largest online game jam in the world, held every April, August, and December.

BOARD GAMES THAT TEACH CODING

Robot Turtles: thinkfun.com/robotturtles

Code Master: thinkfun.com/codemaster

RESOURCES

QR CODE INDEX

ESSENTIAL QUESTIONS

Chapter 1:
What do today's video games have in common with ancient games?

Chapter 2:
How does a video game make you want to keep playing?

Chapter 3:
Why do designers need to think logically about
the games they are designing?

Chapter 4:
How is programming a computer game like baking cookies?

Chapter 5:
Why are the looks and sounds of a game important? Can you
make a game more fun just by changing the look and sound?

Chapter 6:
What can you do now to become a game designer?